A Recent History of Global Imbalances

Edmund Li Sheng

A Recent History of Global Imbalances

palgrave
macmillan

Edmund Li Sheng
School of Political Science and Public
Administration
of Shandong University
Qingdao, China

ISBN 978-981-95-1833-3 ISBN 978-981-95-1834-0 (eBook)
https://doi.org/10.1007/978-981-95-1834-0

This Palgrave Macmillan imprint is published by the registered company Springer Nature Singapore Pte Ltd.
The registered company address is: 152 Beach Road, #21-01/04 Gateway East, Singapore 189721, Singapore

Preface

In an era of unprecedented economic interdependence, global imbalances have emerged as the defining challenge of our time. This book seeks to understand the origins and background of, the difficulties associated with, and solutions to the global imbalances that are becoming increasingly apparent today from the perspective of two major powers: China and the United States. "Global imbalances" mainly refers to international trade imbalances, which are manifested in large trade deficits in some countries and trade surpluses in others. Their roots go back to the post-war Bretton Woods system, which established the US dollar as the global reserve currency and allowed industrialized countries to externalize economic adjustments. However, the acceleration of globalization since the 1990s, combined with China's rise as a manufacturing giant, has transformed these latent imbalances into a systemic fault line. These changes have caused turbulence and uncontrollable instability in global financial markets, international political stability, and national security. This book analyzes the current imbalances between China and the United States, focusing on explaining the mechanism of global imbalances and analyzing their causes theoretically and realistically to find a balanced path for global sustainable development.

This monograph systematically outlines the causes and effects of and countermeasures to global economic imbalances. The main contribution of this approach lies in its endogenous explanation of how current economic models or economic structures systematically lead to imbalances, thus reinforcing the characteristics of the times, such as socioeconomic contradictions, the escalation of competition between major powers, and the return of geopolitics. This monograph reveals the microfoundations of the emergence of the current international situation, analyzes the internal driving forces behind the political adjustments of various countries under the "hard constraints" of economic and material interests, and offers a new analytical dimension for understanding the causes of the current international situation. This monograph also fosters a more fundamental discussion in the field of international political economy: Why do trading partners become strategic rivals? Is the theory of economic peace still valid today? In this discussion, the different theoretical schools of international political economy still debate whether economic and trade relations lead to complementary interests or conflicts of interest, and to what extent conflicts can be resolved once they have arisen. This monograph shows that under certain conditions, economic and trade interdependence can trigger endogenous domestic economic imbalances and international economic frictions (i.e., the inability to coordinate the issue of relative income distribution at the international level), leading to the replacement of liberal logic by realist logic and becoming the dominant logical basis for political adjustments in different countries. This explains many important questions, such as why China and the United States, once the largest trading partners, have moved to strategic confrontation, and why European powers have opted for a certain degree of economic protectionism, which is of interest and great concern to the academic community.

In Chapter 1, "Causes of Global Imbalances," we examine the causes of global imbalances. We begin by analyzing the imbalances in China and the United States, examining in detail their causes from a macroeconomic and microeconomic perspective. We show that the national current account imbalance caused by global imbalances initially affects the national financial market. This in turn leads to capital outflows, which affect the prosperity of the domestic market. However, consumer behavior in the United States leads to a financing gap, both domestically and internationally, and a mismatch between domestic revenues and expenditures. China, for example, has long had a trade surplus and its current account exceeds its borrowing, making it an important global creditor. Therefore, current imbalances in China and the United States contribute to global imbalances.

The differences in national industrial structures and growth models are the fundamental reasons for these imbalances. Industrialized countries tend to rely heavily on high-end manufacturing and services, while shifting labor- and resource-intensive basic industries to developing countries. The division of production activities between industrialized and developing countries leads to trade imbalances. Industrialized countries have a competitive advantage in terms of technological know-how and export technology- and capital-intensive products with high added value. In contrast, developing countries mainly export labor-intensive goods with low added value. This difference in the production pillar leads to trade surpluses and deficits between different countries. While industrialized countries traditionally rely on a consumption-driven growth model, developing countries tend to rely more on external investment and exports as drivers of economic growth and focus on expanding and improving production to increase efficiency and exports. Two different production structures and growth patterns are interacting, which can further exacerbate existing global imbalances. At the same time, this global division of labor has created a structural antagonism between the financial rentier class of industrialized countries and the industrial reserve army of the Global South. Although China has accumulated huge creditor positions, the security dilemma of its dollar-denominated assets and the upward pressure on the renminbi essentially represent a form of covert exploitation by the core countries, such as the US and EU countries to maintain their monetary hegemony.

The development of globalization, the rise of international trade, and the resulting new form of production by multinational corporations, namely outsourcing, are the most direct causes of this growing imbalance. Globalization has led to capital flows, division of labor, diffusion of product technology, development of Internet technology, and development of international logistics, among other outcomes. Since the 1960s, outsourcing production has become a common practice in Western industrialized countries, especially in the United States, as a means of reducing costs. Although outsourcing contributes to the mobility of global factors to some extent, it also contributes to global economic imbalances in many ways. For example, it has led to rising unemployment rates in industrialized countries, industrial collapse, technological spillovers, widening income disparities, and environmental pollution in developing countries. Industrial outsourcing goes beyond mere cost optimization; it constitutes a deliberate strategy used by industrialized countries to maintain technological monopolies and control of global industrial chains. When developing countries try to overcome their "low-end lock-in" through domestic innovation, they quickly encounter containment measures such as technology embargoes (e.g., chip supply cuts) and trade wars. This dynamic equilibrium between dependence and resistance is the real driving force behind the continued development of global economic imbalances.

In Chapter 2, "Deindustrialization and Offshore Outsourcing in the United States," we focus on deindustrialization and outsourcing in the United States. Since the 1950s, the United States has witnessed a societal shift in business and industry, the most prominent features of which are the decline of manufacturing and the rise of the service sector. With the continuous development of the American economy, the service sector, the financial industry, and other tertiary industries have gradually become the main drivers of economic growth. This process triggered the "Rust Belt" phenomenon, in which the Great Lakes industrial region lost more than 8 million manufacturing jobs between 1950 and 2010. In cities like Detroit and Cleveland, the population declined by more than 40%. The decline of communities and escalating social tensions have become an important political issue.

In response to this problem, the Obama administration took a number of policy measures to revitalize manufacturing in the United States and reduce the trade deficit. It encouraged companies to stay in the United States by cutting taxes, promoting business development, expanding infrastructure planning and construction, improving logistics, and reducing operating costs. In addition, it attracted foreign companies through trade policies such as more favorable market access conditions and trade rules for the manufacturing industry in the United States. Thanks to these efforts, the manufacturing industry in the United States has recovered to a certain extent, and the overall effect is reflected in the growth of value added in the manufacturing industry. Specifically, from 2010 to 2021, manufacturing value added in the United States grew at an average annual rate of 1.8%, exceeding pre-financial crisis levels.

In the global economic context, the increase in offshoring in the United States is particularly notable. China, India, Mexico, and other countries with low labor costs are important outsourcing countries. Although outsourcing has reduced costs to a certain extent, it has led to the hollowing out of domestic industries, as well as falling incomes and unemployment. This growth has slowed since Mr. Trump took office.

Through tariff increases and regulatory restructuring, the Trump administration of previous term pursued a rigorous protectionist policy to administratively reshape the industrial landscape. However, by the end of 2019, only 39% of the promised relocations had been implemented. Simply relocating production capacity has proven insufficient to address the structural causes of industrial relocation. As global value chains enter their 3.0 phase, characterized by high interdependence, the United States may need to rethink the nature of the manufacturing renaissance and strike a dynamic balance between openness and protectionism.

In Chapter 3, "Theoretical Explanation and Empirical Analysis of Offshore Outsourcing," we focus on the topic of outsourcing from an economic perspective. The rationality and profitability of outsourcing as a form of production and operation are demonstrated theoretically and empirically. This strategic decision enables companies to effectively reduce production costs, especially in labor-intensive segments, by exploiting the cost advantages of human capital in developing countries and the regulatory advantages of regional trade agreements, thus optimizing the global distribution of resources. At the same time, the non-economic effects of outsourcing, especially social crises and environmental pollution, are taken into account. Using transaction cost theory (TCT) and resource-based theory (RBT), we construct a comprehensive theoretical framework to explain the offshoring behavior of companies. Our theoretical analysis shows that outsourcing can reduce a company's production costs and enable it to make greater use of human, natural, and political resources. However, this outsourcing is associated with major social and environmental problems. These problems are manifested in the relocation of manufacturing, which leads to job losses in domestic firms and an increase in income inequality, in the contraction of the municipal service sector, which puts pressure on social security systems, and in the regulatory arbitrage of environmental standards, which facilitates the relocation of polluting industries to developing countries and causes cross-border pollution effects. Based on multi-country panel data, this chapter examines in particular structural changes in unemployment patterns, the phenomenon of widening skill premiums, the problem of industrial hollowing out, and the existential threats posed by the environmental costs of offshoring to the stability and sustainability of global ecological systems. This analysis provides a solid evidence base for understanding the multidimensional imbalances inherent in globalization processes.

In Chapter 4, "A Global Economy for the Future," we focus on how to overcome global imbalances and find a new model of development. We believe that current industrial structures, economic development models, and international cooperation relations are not sustainable and that we must pursue new paths of industrial development, economic growth, international trade, and cooperation relations. This chapter focuses on industrial rejuvenation, a balanced strategy in the Asia–Pacific region, and friendly outsourcing. Many politicians and decision-makers from both major political parties in the United States have clearly set the goal of reindustrializing the American economy, and numerous government measures have been introduced to this end. The United States is now refocusing on the Indo-Pacific region, strengthening its alliances and partnerships, enhancing its military capabilities to promote economic integration, and promoting shared values and interests. The model of outsourcing activities to suppliers in friendly countries or regions, through friendly outsourcing and strengthening economic relations and cooperation with allies, can reduce supply chain risks to a certain extent and improve the stability and security of their industries, thus becoming a new way of doing international business and production to cope with the effects of outsourcing. The synergy dilemma in implementing these three strategies lies in the difficulty of political interventions in balancing efficiency and security, while the deep interdependence of global industrial chains, characterized by mutual embedding, requires the United States to go beyond zero-sum thinking to rebuild the international order. Whether the United States and even the world can achieve a balance through these three strategies is the focus of this chapter.

In conclusion, we argue that both China and the United States are actively changing current imbalances, but that these changes will inevitably disrupt the division of labor and cooperation that has lasted for nearly half a century, making friction unavoidable. The United States has implemented several policy measures to promote the relocation of manufacturing, but the current dilemma reveals the two constraints of reindustrialization: cost ceilings and technological dependence. Meanwhile, China is leveraging the green transition of the Belt and Road Initiative to reconfigure the discourse power in the value chain, although the resurgence of resource nationalism in developing countries underscores the structural challenges of South–South cooperation. However, constructively, the reform practices of both countries objectively give new impetus to global rebalancing. The Inflation Reduction Act in the United

States stimulated a 37% increase in clean energy investment in 2023, while China's New Productive Forces policy accelerated the growth of industrial robot density. Furthermore, limited cooperation in climate policy and public health shows that "competitive coexistence" is possible, suggesting that strategic rivalry and functional cooperation are not mutually exclusive in the evolving global order.

Qingdao, China Edmund Li Sheng

Contents

List of Figures

CHAPTER 1

Cause of Global Imbalances

As globalization continues to deepen and accelerate, global economic imbalances are becoming ubiquitous and increasingly influencing various dimensions of the global economy. This complex and far-reaching phenomenon undermines the foundations of international trade, affects the flow of goods, services, and capital, and leads to inequalities in both developed and developing economies.

These imbalances are not limited to trade but extend to global financial stability, economic growth patterns, and the broader international political landscape. The scientific and technological revolution, which has dramatically increased global connectivity, the pace of economic development has accelerated rapidly, with some regions benefiting far more than others. Industrialized nations, equipped with advanced technologies and production techniques, have accumulated enormous wealth and resources in a short period. However, many regions are struggling to keep pace and are lagging behind in terms of economic progress and wealth creation. This growing divide has contributed to an imbalance in the distribution of global wealth and exacerbated inequalities in access to technology, capital, and infrastructure.

In the economic sphere, this divergence is particularly evident in the dynamics of international trade. Industrialized countries, thanks to their superior technological and industrial capabilities, exert a dominant influence on major markets and consistently use their advantages to secure

E. Li Sheng, *A Recent History of Global Imbalances*,
https://doi.org/10.1007/978-981-95-1834-0_1

a significant share of global trade. They export high-quality goods and services, thereby consolidating their position at the top of global value chains. In contrast, developing countries remain heavily dependent on exports of primary products and low value-added goods. This dependence on raw materials exacerbates the imbalance in the structure of global trade and makes it difficult for these countries to move up the value chain and compete on equal terms with more developed economies.[1] Furthermore, structural imbalances in trade are exacerbated by the international monetary system, in which the US dollar is dominant. The dominance of the US dollar not only reinforces the influence of US financial policy on the global stage but also makes the global economy vulnerable to changes in US economic policy. Adjustments in US monetary or fiscal policy often send shock waves through international markets, causing volatility that can destabilize economies, particularly in developing regions that rely heavily on trade and financing in dollars.

Although global economic integration theoretically promises more efficient resource allocation and better growth prospects, it has also contributed to widening economic inequalities between nations. This trend is particularly evident in the activities of transnational corporations (TNCs), which have expanded their reach and influence beyond national borders. The global expansion of these corporate giants has facilitated cross-border flows of capital, technology, and labor, widening existing imbalances. TNCs often exploit cost advantages in developing countries by establishing production facilities in regions with lower wages and weaker regulatory environments. Although this strategy may bring short-term economic benefits such as job creation and infrastructure development, it often leads developing countries to play a subordinate role in the global economy. These countries become dependent on foreign capital and technology and are unable to develop the domestic skills needed to compete in higher-value industries. As a result, the global economic divide continues to widen.

In addition, geopolitical strategies play an important role in the formation and exacerbation of global imbalances. Rising trade protectionism, competition for scarce resources, and geopolitical tensions have led to further distortions in the path of balanced global economic development. Countries that adopt protectionist measures often do so in response to

[1] Eichengreen, B. (2010). Global Imbalances and the Lessons of Bretton Woods. The MIT Press.

a perceived threat to their domestic industries, but these measures can disrupt global supply chains and create additional trade imbalances. In addition, the race to control vital resources such as energy, minerals, and technology has distorted the global economic playing field, with wealthier nations often gaining disproportionate access to these important resources.

All of these factors lead to a highly complex and interdependent global economic system that has developed into a systemic risk threatening not only the stability of individual economies but also the sustainability of the global economic order. As the International Monetary Fund (IMF) points out, global current account imbalances have reached historic highs, with persistent deficits in the United States offsetting surpluses in emerging Asian economies. This imbalance is closely linked to the gap between savings and investment. Research shows a negative correlation between income inequality and savings rates: insufficient savings in industrialized countries exacerbate current account deficits, while high savings rates in developing countries reinforce inequalities in global capital flows. While financial globalization facilitates capital mobility, it also spreads such imbalances across the world through complex financial mechanisms, leading to a modern interpretation of the "Triffin dilemma."

1.1 Two Main Sources of Global Imbalances: The United States and China

Since the 1980s, financial crises in both developing and industrialized countries have repeatedly highlighted the profound consequences of global imbalances. These crises have shown that structural weaknesses in the global economic system are not isolated phenomena, but rather interconnected problems that reverberate beyond international borders. The global economy is experiencing increasing real imbalances in savings, investment, and monetary account positions. In addition, financial imbalances, including the prevalence of soft budget constraints, large asset bubbles, and cross-border speculative activities, have reached alarming levels.[2] The 2008 financial crisis further exacerbated these imbalances and exposed deep weaknesses in the global economic order. In the years

[2] Sheng, L. (2014). Income inequality, financial systems, and global imbalances: A theoretical review. Global Policy, 5(1), 311–320. https://doi.org/10.1111/1758-5899.12126.

following the financial crisis, global imbalances continued to worsen, particularly after the tariff war between China and the United States and the COVID-19 pandemic, which had serious consequences for the international economic system. The imbalances between the United States and China are highlighted by their tariff war. Since 2018, the United States has imposed tariffs on Chinese imports, and China has retaliated with its own tariffs. This tariff war has not only reduced the volume of trade between the two countries but has also disrupted global supply chains and increased economic uncertainty. The tariff war has also had a major impact on the global economy. It has affected many countries and influenced global economic imbalances. The COVID-19 pandemic acted as a shock multiplier, exacerbating existing imbalances in global trade, capital flows, and financial markets. This crisis led to a drastic drop in global demand, supply chain disruptions, and rising budget deficits, highlighting the fragility of the global economic structure. These growing imbalances can largely be attributed to the macroeconomic policies and structural characteristics of major economies, particularly the United States and China.

Global current account imbalances and associated net capital flows have been at the center of political debate in recent years. In the wake of the financial crisis, many observers and policymakers identified them as a key factor in the crisis.[3] In 2005, Ben Bernanke put forward the "global savings glut" hypothesis, positing a causal link between three phenomena: the constantly growing current account deficit in the United States, the massive surpluses in emerging economies (particularly in East Asia and oil-exporting countries), and the global decline in long-term real interest rates. He argued that the post-crisis decline in investment, rising oil revenues, and high savings rates in emerging economies—due to underdeveloped financial systems and weak social safety nets—turned these economies from net borrowers to net savers. This shift led to large capital inflows into industrialized countries such as the United States, which depressed interest rates and exacerbated imbalances.[4]

[3] For example, Bernanke (2009a), Council of Economic Advisers (2009), Dunaway (2009), Economist (2009), Eichengreen (2009), King (2010), Kohn (2010), Krugman (2009), and Portes (2009). Elements of this story are also found in Eichengreen (2009).

[4] Bernanke, B. S. (2007). Global imbalances: Recent developments and prospects. Bundesbank lecture, Berlin, Germany.

As the world's largest economy, the United States has long maintained a pattern of low savings and high consumption, which has directly contributed to its high current account deficit.[5] This structural imbalance is driven by the country's consumption-oriented economic model, in which private household consumption accounts for a disproportionately large share of GDP, supported by high debt and low personal savings. At the same time, China, as a major emerging market, has contributed to global imbalances by accumulating large foreign exchange reserves through its high savings and export-oriented growth strategy.[6] China's accumulation of reserves, particularly in US dollars, is a direct consequence of its trade surplus and export-oriented policies. This divergence in the economic strategies of the two nations has contributed significantly to the persistence of global economic imbalances and makes it difficult to achieve balance in the international financial system.

The main concern is that the long-standing current account deficit of the United States is contributing significantly to global imbalances. The country's decades-long structural deficit reflects deep-rooted macroeconomic dynamics, including the role of the US dollar as the primary international reserve currency and persistent domestic consumption that exceeds production. As a result, the United States depends on importing excess savings from emerging economies, particularly Asia and oil-exporting countries, to finance its growth. This dependence not only perpetuates global financial imbalances but also contributes to the "exorbitant privilege" enjoyed by the United States in global capital markets.[7] The cyclical pattern of deficit spending, coupled with capital inflows from high-saving regions, creates a self-reinforcing mechanism that amplifies systemic vulnerabilities in the global economy.

The current account, also called the cash account, is an important part of the balance of payments, which records all non-financial transactions between a country or region and other countries over a given period. The current account reflects the flow of money between a country or region and other countries or regions arising from economic activities

[5] Bernanke, B. S. (2005). The global saving glut and the US current account deficit. In The Sandridge Lecture: Virginia Association of Economics, Richmond.

[6] Zhang, Y. (2012). China's high savings rate: Causes, prospects, and policies. China & Weltwirtschaft, 20(2), 1–18.

[7] Davis, C. (2006). US hegemony, China, and the US current account deficit. Pacific Focus, 21(2), 7–44. https://doi.org/10.1111/j.1976-5118.2006.tb00319.x.

such as goods, services, income, and current transfers over a given period. It is a key component of national accounts and an important indicator of a country's economic vitality and international competitiveness. The current account consists mainly of the following four core components:

Goods: Covers all physical goods imported and exported, such as general goods, goods for processing, raw materials, consumer goods, and capital goods. This is the most intuitive and understandable part of the current account.
Services: Including transportation, tourism, communication services, construction services, insurance services, financial services, education, consulting, and other intangible economic activities. With the continuous development of the global economy, the status of service items in the current account is gradually increasing.
Income: Mainly refers to remuneration obtained from the international mobility of factors of production (such as labor and capital), including employee remuneration (such as the income of overseas workers) and investment income (such as interest and dividends).
Frequent transfers: One-way financial flows with no direct return, such as government foreign aid, remittances from the diaspora to family back home, donations, and inheritances. These transactions usually take place between residents and non-residents and involve changes in ownership of real resources or financial items without equivalent exchange.

The rise and persistence of external imbalances since the early 1990s, as well as the resurgence of the intertemporal approach to current account balances, have led to a new wave of empirical studies that attempt to explain the determinants of current account balances in a context of increasing geographical dispersion.[8] According to Mann (2002),[9] we can identify up to four representations of the current account:

$$CA_t \equiv S_t - I_t \tag{1.1}$$

[8] Camarero, M., Carrion-i-Silvestre, J. L., & Tamarit, C. (2021). External imbalances from a GVAR perspective. The World Economy, 44(11), 3202–3245. https://doi.org/10.1111/twec.13122.

[9] Mann, C. L. (2002). Perspectives on the US current account deficit and sustainability. Journal of Economic Perspectives, 16(3), 131–152.

$$CA_t \equiv GDP_t - AB_t \tag{1.2}$$

$$CA_t \equiv (NFA_t - NFA_{t-1}) \tag{1.3}$$

$$CA_t \equiv NX_t \tag{1.4}$$

where CA_t, is the current account (assuming that net foreign income and unilateral transfers are zero) and S_t, I_t, and AB_t represent savings, investment, and absorption, respectively; $NFA_t = A_t - L_t$ is the net foreign asset position (with A_t indicating assets and L_t indicating liabilities), and NX_t is the trade balance. Thus, the above expressions are accounting identities linking the current account and the accumulation of foreign assets, the trade balance, savings, investment, income, and absorption. Following Mann (2002), these identities actually represent three perspectives on the current account, which are interpreted in terms of potential adjustment channels in the event of a shock. Identities (1) and (2) correspond to the domestic perspective, which is based on national income and production. The international perspective, which is based on flows and stocks of financial assets, is represented by identity (3), while "identity" (4) refers to the adjustment channel based on trade in goods and services. Although these identities are simple, they illustrate the diverse relationships among all of the macroeconomic variables involved.

Figure 1.1 shows that the current account balance, with horizontal axis representing year and vertical axis measuring current account in billion US$, in the United States is consistently in deficit. This deficit increased significantly, especially after 1980, reaching its peak around 2022. The United States had accumulated a deficit of US$54 billion during World War II, which was equivalent to 25% of the total economy. In the post-war decades, the country reduced its debt burden relative to GDP, not through budget surpluses but through rapid economic expansion that outpaced debt growth. In the 1980s, President Ronald Reagan passed several tax cut measures, such as the Economic Recovery Tax Act of 1981. However, he did nothing to reduce spending. As a result, deficits began to explode again. Since then, the country has experienced a series of large deficits and growing debt, most recently with the 2008 recession and the COVID-19 pandemic.[10] In 2023, the current account deficit in the United States decreased to approximately $818.8 billion, a 15.7% decline from 2022. This decline was primarily due to a significant reduction in the goods deficit, as exports of goods declined slightly while imports fell more sharply. An important factor behind these changes is the aftermath of the extensive fiscal stimulus programs adopted during the pandemic, which initially increased the deficit. Large-scale fiscal interventions by the US government, such as direct payments to households, temporarily increased disposable income, leading to higher consumption and imports. Due to the expiration of pandemic-related support measures in 2023, the plan caused the current account deficit to peak in 2022.

Extensive research shows a clear link between the current account deficit and the country's high-income inequality and low savings rate. The United States has a service-oriented economic structure, which has enabled it to occupy an important position in the global services market.

Fig. 1.1 Current account deficit in the United States (billions of US dollars) https://data.worldbank.org/indicator/BN.CAB.XOKA.CD?end=2023&locations=US&start=1970&view=chart (*Source* World Bank Group)

[10] Hannah, L. (2023, December 21). The US deficit is large—but does it matter? We asked an economist. GBH. https://www.wgbh.org/people/hannah-loss; https://www.wgbh.org/news/local/2023-12-21/the-us-deficit-is-big-but-does-it-matter-we-asked-an-economist.

This structure has fostered its growth through technological innovation and attracted significant global investments. Nevertheless, the successful deindustrialization of the United States, which has led to the outsourcing of many manufacturing industries and a subsequent reliance on imports to meet domestic demand, has also resulted in significant trade deficits, growing inequality, and high unemployment rates.[11] Inequalities between low- and high-income groups are increasing. However, a highly liberalized financial system and a growing market-based banking sector enable low and middle-income groups to improve or stabilize their living standards by borrowing domestically.[12] A spending deficit that curbs the increase in consumption inequality inevitably leads to a reduction in the overall savings rate, which in turn weighs on the current account.[13] In this context, consumption inequality in the United States is significantly less pronounced than inequality in income distribution, while the propensity to save domestically remains relatively low. Such a policy has enabled the United States to maintain a growing current account deficit while domestic consumer demand has remained robust. To mitigate the deficit and increase capital liquidity, the United States used the structural influence of the dollar to encourage East Asian countries to increase their dollar-denominated assets by attracting foreign capital and issuing government bonds,[14] thereby allowing the United States to reduce its savings and transfer risk to other countries based on the credibility of the dollar.

One of the most important factors exacerbating global imbalances is the dominance of the US dollar as the world's main reserve currency. Since the end of World War II and the establishment of the Bretton Woods system, the dollar has maintained its position as the backbone of the international monetary system. More than 60% of global reserves

[11] Arnold, L. G., & Riley, J. G. (2009). On the possibility of credit rationing in the Stiglitz-Weiss model. American Economic Review, 99(5), 2012–2021.

[12] Yin, Y. C., & Sheng, L. (2021). Theoretical considerations on global imbalances: An inequality perspective. Argumenta Oeconomica, 46(1), 169–181. https://doi.org/10.15611/aoe.2021.1.08.

[13] Brown, C. (2008). Inequality, consumer credit, and the savings puzzle. In M. Sawyer (Ed.), New Directions in Modern Economics. Edward Elgar Publishing.

[14] Vermeiren, M. (2010). Global imbalances and the contradictions of US monetary hegemony. Journal of International Relations and Development. https://doi.org/10.1057/jird.2009.36.

are held in dollars, giving the United States significant structural advantages, including the ability to easily finance its current account deficit by issuing dollar-denominated debt. Countries around the world hold enormous reserves of US Treasury securities, enabling the United States to externalize much of the financial risks associated with its persistent trade and budget deficits. This phenomenon has enabled the country to borrow cheaply and thus stimulate domestic consumption and investment, but it also makes the global economy dependent on US economic policy and contributes to the persistence of global imbalances.

As the world's most important reserve currency, US monetary policy influences global capital flows and thus global balance sheets. Using a structural Vector Autoregression VAR model that incorporates production, inflation, interest rates, oil price inflation, the current account balance, total consumption and investment, and the real effective exchange rate, Barnett and Straub (2008) show that monetary policy shocks played a decisive role in the deterioration of the US current account balance between 1970 and 2006. When breaking down the variance of the forecast error, monetary policy shocks accounted for over 60% of the one-year forecast.[15]

The Mundell trilemma, or incompatibility triangle, describes a limited relationship between exchange rates, monetary policy, and capital flows. It refers to the impossibility of having perfect capital mobility, an autonomous monetary policy, and a fixed exchange rate simultaneously. In an environment of total capital mobility, the interest rate cannot simultaneously serve an external and an internal target.[16] It is in this context that monetary authorities make their decisions, and the dynamics of global liquidity therefore also depend on these relationships. Monetary easing in one economy can create a shock in another economy through interest rate cuts. Ceteris paribus, such a monetary policy shock widens the interest rate differential between the two countries, making capital flows more attractive. This promotes the appreciation of the second country's currency and reduces its price competitiveness. To limit the negative effects on the real economy and financial market bubbles and to avoid

[15] Barnett, A., & Straub, R. (2008). What drives fluctuations in the US current account? December 2008SSRN Electronic Journal.

[16] Gourinchas, P. O., & Rey, H. (2012). Global imbalances and global liquidity. In National Bureau of Economic Research, Asia Economic Policy Conference (pp. 28–30). Federal Reserve Bank of San Francisco.

sudden and large capital outflows, the monetary authority of the second country must therefore also lower its key interest rate. The interest rate differential between the two countries then returns to its original equilibrium. In short, a liquidity shock caused by one country triggers a reaction in other countries, leading to an increase in global liquidity, which in turn affects the global balance.

These mechanisms between national monetary policy and global liquidity dynamics are illustrated in Fig. 1.1, which considers three groups of countries. Group 1 includes only the United States (US). The second group includes other advanced countries, namely the United Kingdom (UK), the euro area (EA), Japan (JP), and Canada (CN). Finally, the third group consists of emerging economies (EMEs). Faced with global liquidity inflows, emerging economies are accumulating foreign exchange reserves to counter large capital inflows and upward pressure on their currencies, and then reinvesting these reserves in safe assets such as US Treasuries. In this context, Caballero (2006) argues that a shortage of assets in emerging economies leads to a strong demand for US assets, so the prospect of an asset shortage could explain low real interest rates and global imbalances(Fig. 1.2).[17]

The United States can maintain highly unequal domestic income and consumption patterns through policy coordination and exchange rate interventions, which simultaneously undermine international credibility and the value of the dollar and expose the United States to the Triffin dilemma through rising current account deficits.[18] To eliminate the current imbalance, it is essential to increase US national savings,[19] thereby reducing the deficit and improving the competitiveness of the US dollar. The relationship between national savings, investment, and economic growth is crucial. Growth theories attribute an important role to the increase in savings and investment in the growth process. For example, the Harrod–Domar model emphasizes the benefits of investment for production growth. This suggests that higher savings and investment are

[17] Caballero, R. J. (2006). On the macroeconomics of asset scarcity. NBER working paper no. 12753.

[18] Mian, A., & Sufi, A. (2009). The consequences of mortgage credit expansion: Evidence from the 2007 mortgage default crisis. Quarterly Journal of Economics, 124(4), 1449–1496. https://doi.org/10.1162/qjec.2009.124.4.1449.

[19] Kenen, P. (2005). The stabilization of the international monetary system. Journal of Policy Modeling, 27(4), 487–493. https://doi.org/10.1016/j.jpolmod.2005.04.014.

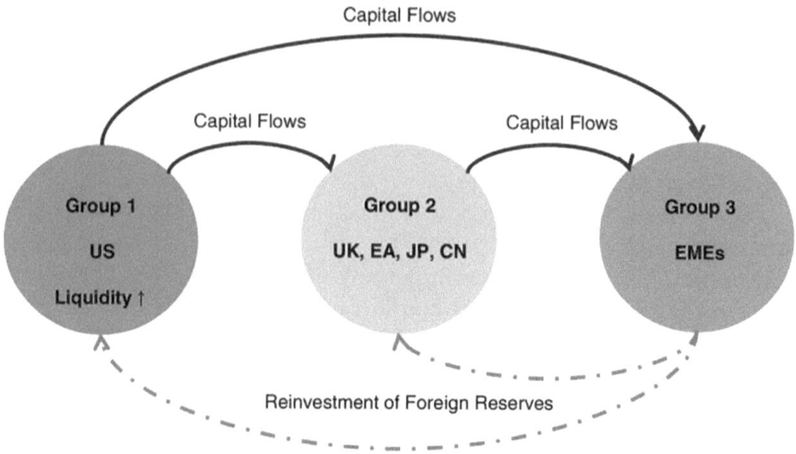

Fig. 1.2 US monetary shock and global liquidity spillovers (*Source* Gourinchas, P. O., & Rey, H. (2012). Global imbalances and global liquidity. In National Bureau of Economic Research, *Asia Economic Policy Conference* (pp. 28–30). Federal Reserve Bank of San Francisco. https://www.researchgate.net/publication/236211772_Global_Imbalances_and_Global_Liquidity)

crucial for long-term economic growth. In contrast, low savings lead to insufficient domestic investment, low economic growth, rising foreign debt, and unemployment.[20] Higher national savings can lead to greater investment in production activities, which can increase the economy's production capacity and thus its growth potential over time. To counter a declining national savings rate, policies aimed at reducing government deficits, encouraging private savings through tax incentives or retirement programs, and improving incomes through measures that stimulate economic growth and job creation can be effective. The United States now urgently needs to strengthen its economic resilience by promoting reindustrialization through targeted tax incentives. This strategy should focus on boosting exports and reducing dependence on imports, while levying sufficiently high taxes to curb financialization. At the same time,

[20] Abu, N., & Karim, M. Z. A. (2016). The relationship between foreign direct investment, domestic savings, domestic investment, and economic growth: The case of Sub-Saharan Africa. Society and Economy, 38(2), 193–217. https://doi.org/10.1556/204.2016.38.2.4.

structural imbalances in the current account must be addressed by curbing debt-financed overconsumption and creating incentives for household savings. It is crucial that working-class wages remain disproportionately low relative to labor productivity in surplus countries. Raising wages would not only reduce income and consumption inequality but also boost aggregate demand, thereby reducing the dependence of domestic growth on foreign markets.

China is increasingly perceived by nations and policymakers as a critical force contributing to global imbalances in the current international economic landscape. Its rapid economic development, coupled with its unique economic structure and political orientation, makes it a central player in the global economic landscape, particularly in relation to global imbalances. China has experienced rapid growth and has become a key location for global manufacturing, mainly due to its enormous labor resources and relatively low production costs.

In 1980, China ranked seventh behind Italy, but it overtook the United States in 2011 as the world's largest manufacturer of industrial goods.[21] This has enabled the country to export a significant amount of goods to various global markets, leading to the accumulation of substantial trade surpluses and influencing the global trade landscape. Import and export data for the last two decades show that China has achieved a trade surplus and that its import and export balance is growing. In 2022, China was the world's second largest economy by GDP (in current US dollars), the largest exporter, and the second largest importer.[22] Its main exports are radio and television equipment ($272 billion), integrated circuits ($212 billion), computers ($181 billion), office machine parts ($111 billion), and semiconductors ($70.2 billion), which are mainly exported to the United States ($551 billion), Hong Kong ($276 billion), Japan ($178 billion), Germany ($152 billion), and South Korea ($150

[21] Karel, E., Alan, H., & Martin, L. (2013, June 1). A new era for China's manufacturing industry. MeKinsey&Company. https://www.mckinsey.com/our-people/karel-eloot; https://www.mckinsey.com/capabilities/operations/our-insights/a-new-era-for-manufacturing-in-china.

[22] China National Bureau of Statistics (2024, July). China (CHN) Exports, Imports and Trading Partners. The Observatory of Economic Complexity. https://oec.world/en/profile/country/chn.

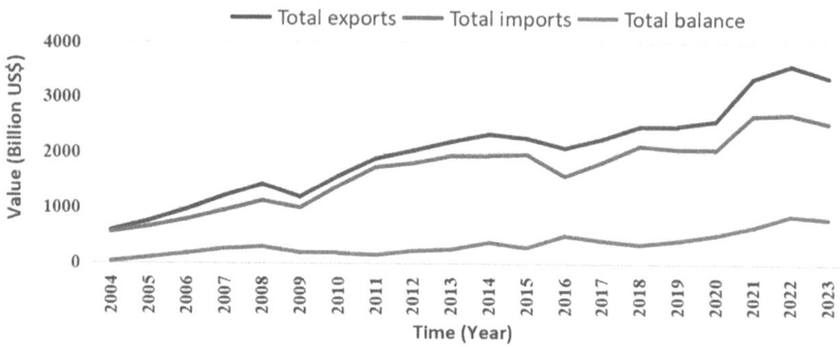

Fig. 1.3 China's import and export trade data (millions of US$) (*Source* China National Bureau of Statistics. http://data.mofcom.gov.cn/hwmy/imexmonth.shtml)

billion).[23] As a result, China's trade surplus has reached an all-time high and is likely to rise even further (Fig. 1.3).

In addition, China's high savings rate continues to contribute significantly to global economic imbalances. Studies show that current account surpluses in several emerging economies are contributing to fueling the credit boom and risk-taking in the large deficit advanced countries at the center of the crisis by putting significant downward pressure on global interest rates and/or simply financing the boom in these countries (the "excess savings" view).[24] China has consistently had one of the highest national savings rates in the world, far exceeding both the global average and that of other emerging economies. Historically, national savings have been high since the 1980s, at around 35%–40% of GDP. After China joined the World Trade Organization (WTO) in 2001, savings peaked at 52% of GDP in 2008. After the 2008 global financial crisis, savings gradually declined to 46% in 2017, compared with the global average of

[23] China National Bureau of Statistics (2024, July). China (CHN) Exports, Imports and Trading Partners. The Observatory of Economic Complexity. https://oec.world/en/profile/country/chn.

[24] Borio, C., & Disyatat, P. (2010). Global imbalances and the financial crisis: Reassessing the role of international finance. Asian Economic Policy Review, 5(2), 198–216. https://doi.org/10.1111/j.1748-3131.2010.01163.x.

20% and 15% for emerging economies.[25] The latest data for 2022 show that China's savings rate is around 45.75% of GDP.[26] This figure is still more than double the global average of around 20%, and it is significantly higher than the 15%–25% typical of emerging economies. The main causes include China's rapid economic growth, its accession to the WTO, rising corporate profits, changes in living incomes, the pension system, social benefits, and demographic changes.[27] This persistently high savings rate continues to contribute to global economic imbalances, as it generates large current account surpluses and substantial foreign exchange reserves, which in turn have far-reaching implications for the dynamics of global trade, foreign exchange markets, and capital flows.

The imbalance between consumption and savings in China is a complex economic phenomenon that encompasses many economic theories. From the perspective of structural economics, the imbalance in the economic structure is one of the most important reasons for the imbalance between consumption and savings. In the context of an open economy, the imbalance of economic structure mainly includes the imbalance of investment and consumption structure, industrial structure, and financial structure. The imbalance in the structure of investment and consumption is manifested in a high savings rate and an insufficient consumption rate. This imbalance leads to an uncoordinated production structure within industries, reduces the efficiency of the industrial structure, and then has a negative impact on the real economy and the financial system. In China, the imbalance in the structure of investment and consumption has different effects in different geographical areas due to uneven regional economic development.

In addition, some important variables in the financial system influence consumption, savings, and investment. Income distribution is an important factor influencing consumption and savings. The theory of income distribution states that if income is distributed unfairly or there is too large

[25] Zhang, M. L., Brooks, M. R., Ding, D., Ding, H., He, H., Lu, J., & Mano, R. (2018). China's High Savings: Drivers, Prospects, and Policy. International Monetary Fund.

[26] CEIC. (2025). China Gross Savings Ratio. CEIC data. https://www.ceicdata.com.cn/en/indicator/china/gross-savings-rate.

[27] Yang, D. T., Zhang, J., & Zhou, S. (2012). Why are savings rates so high in China? In Fan and Morck: Capitalizing China (pp. 249–278). University of Chicago Press.

a gap between high and low incomes, low-income groups will have insufficient purchasing power, while high-income groups will be more inclined to save than to spend. This inequality in income distribution can hamper the growth of overall consumer demand and thus exacerbate the problem of excess savings and insufficient consumption.

In China, the link between the corporate sector and the resident sector in terms of property rights is weak, meaning that companies are state-owned and their business objectives do not align with the preferences of residents. This hinders the flexible transfer of resources between companies and residents, resulting in residents receiving virtually no dividend income from the corporate sector.[28] This inadequate distribution of income is also one of the reasons for the lack of consumption and excess savings of Chinese residents.

The life cycle hypothesis and the permanent income hypothesis explain the relationship between savings and consumption from the perspective of consumer behavior. These hypotheses state that consumers control their consumption depending on their expected life cycle income and their permanent income.[29] However, due to factors such as the imperfection of the social security system, the deterioration of the consumption environment, and residents' expectations of future income instability, Chinese residents may be more inclined to increase their savings to cope with future uncertainties. From the perspective of the savings–investment identity, the difference between domestic savings and domestic investment leads to a trade surplus or deficit. In China, the high long-term savings rate and the relatively insufficient investment rate lead to a net outflow of domestic resources and the emergence of a trade surplus.

However, this trade surplus does not effectively translate into an increase in domestic consumer demand, but instead exacerbates the problem of excess savings and insufficient consumption. At the same time, the uncertainty of the international trade environment affects the imbalance between consumption and savings in China. A decline in foreign demand will lead to a decline in exports, which in turn will

[28] Sheng, L. (2014). Income inequality, financial systems, and global imbalances: A theoretical review. Global Politics, 5(3), 311–320. https://doi.org/10.1111/1758-5899.12126.

[29] Modigliani, F., & Brumberg, R. (1954). Utility analysis and the consumption function: An interpretation of cross-section data. In K. Kurihara (Ed.), Postkeynesian Economics (pp. 388–436). Rutgers University Press.

affect production and employment in domestic companies and further hamper the growth of consumer demand. Political factors and social and cultural traditions are also important factors influencing the imbalance between consumption and savings in China. For example, the government invests too much in capital formation, while the share of private investment is too low, which undermines the driving effect of investment on long-term economic development. In addition, influenced by traditional culture, Chinese people generally have a high propensity to save and are risk averse, which also exacerbates the problem of excess savings and insufficient consumption (Fig. 1.4).

High savings are the reason for China's external and internal imbalances. Low national savings can be a barrier to financing economic development, and high savings can also distort the structure of the economy and lead to unsustainable growth and external imbalances. High private savings force people to save heavily for retirement or may be a sign of poor corporate governance, allowing companies to retain and

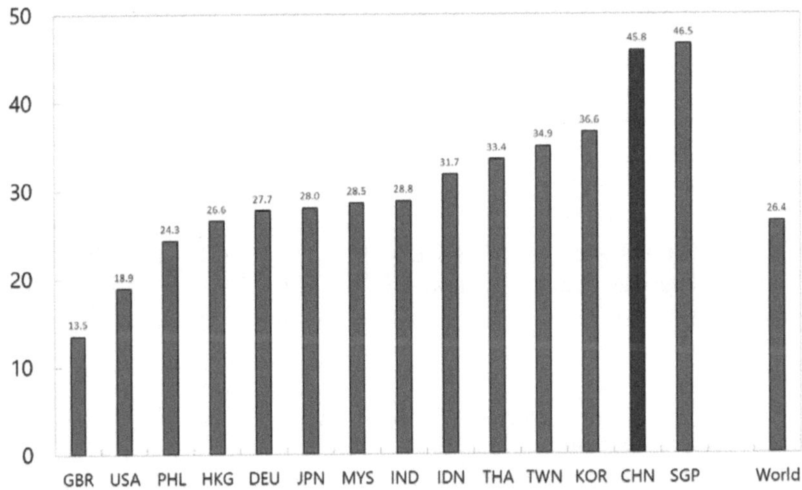

Fig. 1.4 National savings rate (2017) (as a % of GDP) (*Source* Zhang, M. L., Brooks, M. R., Ding, D., Ding, H., He, H., Lu, J., & Mano, R. (2018). *China's High Savings: Drivers, Prospects, and Policies.* International Monetary Fund)

reinvest most of their profits.[30] Domestic savings habits and the inadequacies of the social security system have led domestic residents to save rather than consume. As a result, the domestic consumer market has remained relatively inadequate, while economic growth has become more dependent on investment and exports, further increasing the trade surplus and income disparities. The consequence of rigorous regulatory measures is that China's domestic financial market remains underdeveloped. Consequently, the wealth accumulated by high-income groups cannot be effectively converted into capital for investment in infrastructure and other capital-intensive projects. Furthermore, these groups are unable to provide loans to low-income individuals for consumption purposes. A considerable volume of excess savings is diverted from China to the United States, Europe, and other countries through current account deficits, effectively contributing to capital outflows.[31] At the same time, the Chinese banking and financial system is not yet fully developed and the legal framework is not yet solid.[32] Foreign investment can easily trigger asset bubbles in China, and financial speculation can significantly harm the real economy, thereby exacerbating inequality and high savings.

At the international level, China's persistent trade surpluses and its role as the United States' main creditor have led to the accumulation of huge foreign exchange reserves, particularly in US dollars. According to recent data, China remains one of the largest holders of US debt, consolidating its role as a key financier of the American economy. Although these reserves give China significant global financial influence, they also hinder the internationalization of the Chinese yuan.[33] The huge volume of US dollar reserves increases China's dependence on the US dollar-dominated global financial system and limits its ability to promote the yuan as an international currency. This dependence also forces China to

[30] Blanchard, O. J., & Milesi-Ferretti, G. M. (2010). Global imbalances: In the middle of the stream? Available at SSRN 1525542.

[31] Caballero, R., Farhi, E., & Gourinchas, P. O. (2008). An equilibrium model for global imbalances and low interest rates. American Economic Review, 98(1), 358–393.

[32] Sheng, L., & Zhang, Z. (2021). Revisiting global imbalances: A comparative analysis of income and consumption inequality. Economics & Politics, 34, 382–390. https://doi.org/10.1111/ecpo.12202.

[33] Vernengo, M. (2021). The consolidation of dollar hegemony after the collapse of Bretton Woods: Bringing power back in. Review of Political Economy, 33(4), 529–551. https://doi.org/10.1080/09538259.2021.1950966.

assume some of the financial risks associated with the global hegemony of the US dollar. As the largest holder of US debt, China is not only exposed to potential fluctuations in the value of the US dollar but also indirectly supports the structural dominance of the US dollar in international markets. This structural imbalance hinders China's long-term goal of expanding the yuan's global influence and limits its ability to assert greater autonomy in international financial affairs. Another reason for its high reserves is self-insurance,[34] which may be reasonable at the national level but is inefficient from a global perspective compared with alternative arrangements such as the establishment of credit lines, reserve pooling agreements, swap lines, or other forms of insurance.

A trade surplus, a key term in international trade, occurs when a country's total exports of goods and services exceed its imports over a given period (usually one year). Trade surpluses have many effects on the economy. In positive terms, a trade surplus means that a country is highly competitive in the international market and can produce and export a large number of advantageous goods and services. This helps to promote the development and modernization of domestic industries, improve production efficiency, and drive technological innovation. At the same time, the trade surplus generates significant foreign exchange earnings and increases the country's foreign exchange reserves. Adequate foreign exchange reserves are of great importance for stabilizing the exchange rate of the domestic currency, improving international solvency, and coping with external economic risks. In addition, the flourishing of the export industry can create more jobs and promote economic growth and social stability.

However, persistent surpluses are associated with risks. Consistently high trade surpluses can lead to trade conflicts. Other countries may perceive the exports as a burden on their domestic industries and take protectionist measures, such as the introduction of tariffs, which would have a negative impact on their exports. In addition, trade surpluses can lead to increased upward pressure on the domestic currency. Currency appreciation weakens the price competitiveness of export products and has a certain impact on the export industry. Furthermore, long-term trade surpluses can make the economy overly dependent on exports, and once

[34] Mendoza, E. G., Quadrini, V., & Rios-Rull, J. V. (2009). Financial integration, financial development, and global imbalances. Journal of Political Economy, 117(3), 371–416. https://www.journals.uchicago.edu/doi/10.1086/599706.

demand in the international market changes, the domestic economy may face greater pressure to adjust.

As a country with a long history of trade surpluses, China's trade surplus is due to a number of reasons. First, the advantages of low-cost production, attributable to abundant labor and integrated supply chains, improve the price competitiveness of Chinese goods worldwide. Second, since its reform and opening up since 1979, the Chinese government has promoted the development of an export-oriented economy, which has led to a gradual shift of Chinese industries toward labor—and resource-intensive sectors and the emergence of an export-oriented economic growth model. China occupies an important position in the global supply chain and has become an important production and assembly location for companies around the world. This makes it possible to import a large number of intermediate products into China and export them as finished products after processing, thereby increasing the volume of exports. In terms of monetary policy, the RMB exchange rate has remained relatively stable in recent years and is sometimes considered relatively undervalued. This helps to increase the competitiveness of exports, which in turn increases the trade surplus.

China's persistent trade surplus has profound implications for global imbalances. As the world's second largest economy, China's continued trade surplus has strengthened trade with other countries and promoted the process of global economic integration. Chinese exports reduce costs and increase prosperity for consumers worldwide. At the same time, trade cooperation between China and other countries has promoted economic cooperation and joint development.

However, advancing global economic integration also poses certain challenges. The price competitiveness of Chinese exports can put pressure on similar industries in other countries, leading to a gradual decline of these industries and job losses in some countries. Such dynamics could trigger protectionist tendencies in some countries and increase the risk of trade conflicts. Meanwhile, global economic integration is progressing and strengthening the interdependence of the global economy. China's persistent trade surplus is putting economic pressure on some of its trading partners. These countries may view Chinese exports as a shock to their domestic industries and take protectionist measures to restrict Chinese exports. Some countries could, for example, raise tariffs, set quotas, or introduce other trade barriers to restrict imports of Chinese products. The rise of trade protectionism has a negative impact on the global economy. In addition, protectionist measures will lead to an increase in trade barriers and hamper the flow of international trade. This could lead to a decline in the volume of global trade and hamper global economic growth. Trade protectionism can also lead to trade wars and trade conflicts, exacerbating tensions in international relations. This could undermine the international economic order and affect the stability and development of the global economy.

China's persistent trade surplus has increased its foreign exchange reserves, gradually improving its status in the international monetary system. However, this also poses a challenge to the stability of the international monetary system. First, the large size of China's foreign exchange reserves has gradually increased its influence in the international financial market. This may affect the monetary and exchange rate policies of other countries and increase the complexity of the international monetary system. Second, persistent trade surpluses can lead to imbalances in the global economy and increase the instability of global growth. China's export-oriented economic growth model makes the Chinese economy overly dependent on exports, and once international market demand changes, the domestic economy may be under significant adjustment pressure.[35] Such dependence could jeopardize China's sustainable economic development. Global economic imbalances can also lead to economic problems in other countries. Some countries may face challenges such as debt problems or slower economic growth due to trade deficits. This can lead to fluctuations and uncertainties in the global economy and affect its stability and development.

In the wake of a global financial crisis, China's economy is facing a number of challenges. Responses to these challenges are likely to evolve toward systemic structural adjustments. After more than a decade of massive public investment in infrastructure, returns from similar projects are likely to decline. Due to external pressures, China is likely to experience relatively modest export growth in the future and strive for a more balanced current account. These plans mean that China will increasingly rely on strong domestic demand to ensure sustainable growth and structural changes from its previous investment—and export-oriented growth strategy. To alleviate its predicament, China is also actively taking

[35] Fall, M. K. (2017). Trade flows versus capital flows: Are China's trade surpluses overestimated? International Economic Journal, 31(3), 448–461.

measures to mitigate global imbalances. By promoting economic restructuring, strengthening the development of the domestic demand market, and encouraging consumption upgrading, China has sought to shift economic growth from an export—and investment-driven model to one coordinated by consumption, investment, and exports.

The Chinese economy has entered a "new normal" phase characterized by structural changes toward sustainable growth and a GDP growth rate that has stabilized at around 6%, while consumption has become the main driver of economic expansion. The contribution of consumer spending to GDP growth in 2021 reached 65.4%.[36] At the same time, strengthening economic cooperation with other nations, further developing the multilateral trading system, and seeking a rebalancing of the global economy are inevitable measures. However, this process will continue to lead to growing divergences of interests between China and the United States, with the implementation of trade protectionist measures by both parties posing a threat to the stability of the international economic system and contributing to a worsening of global imbalances.

1.2 The Impact of Different National Production Structures and Growth Patterns on Global Imbalances

In theory, the equilibrium of the balance of payments is a fundamental goal of macroeconomic external equilibrium. In contrast, current account imbalances have become a prominent feature of the global economic landscape, reflecting a divergence between theory and real economic activity. Specifically, since the 1990s, there has been a global phenomenon of long-term current account deficits in certain industrialized countries, including the United States and the United Kingdom, while persistent current account surpluses have been observed in certain emerging Asian economies and oil-exporting countries. Given the accelerated development of communication and information technology, increasing trade liberalization, transregional international division of labor, and synergistic cooperation have emerged as new means of trade in the global economy.

[36] Zhang Y.R. (2024). Research on consumption-driven economics under the new normal of the economy. (Jing ji xin chang tai xia xiao fei qu dong de jing ji xue yan jiu). Investment and Cooperation, 7, 177–179.

Furthermore, the growing maturity and sophistication of the new international division of labor are having a profound impact on the structure of the global economy and trade.[37] From this perspective, the production structures and growth patterns of different countries exert a complex and profound influence on global imbalances. Differences in production structures lead to an unequal division of labor between countries in the global economy, which in turn affects trade balances and resource allocation.[38] According to Keynesian structural theory, the problem of global imbalances has both a supply and a demand side. The supply side reflects the new production paradigm that underpins neoliberal globalization, while the demand side reflects the Keynesian theory of hegemonic currencies.[39] This also includes the political economy, which explains how politics enabled the emergence of these new global arrangements of supply and demand.[40]

In terms of production structure, industrialized countries generally rely on high-value manufacturing and the service sector to drive economic growth. Since the 1970s, these countries have gradually shifted their economic structure, moving from a dominant manufacturing industry to services and high-tech industries. According to Eurostat, growth in the service sector accounts for more than 70% of economic growth in the 28-member European Union. Innovation in the service sector has become a new engine of economic growth, particularly in emerging areas such as the digital economy, cloud computing, and artificial intelligence. These emerging areas not only promote the rapid development of the service industry but also stimulate the expansion and development of corresponding industrial chains and give new impetus to economic growth.

[37] Wei, R.Q, Su, H., Wang, S.Y. & Zheng L.K. (2020). Research on the impact of global value chain division of labor on global imbalances: A perspective based on the mode of GVC participation under the global production decomposition model. (quan qiu jia zhi lian fen gong dui quan qiu shi heng de ying xiang yan jiu--ji yu quan qiu sheng chan fen jie mo xing xia GVC can yu fang shi de shi jiao). International Finance Studies, 4, 3–12. doi: https://doi.org/10.16475/j.cnki.1006-1029.2020.04.00.

[38] Sachs, J. D. (2011). Achieving sustainable global growth. In S. Anand, P. Segal, & J. E. Stiglitz (Eds.), Global Development: A Brief History. World Bank Publications.

[39] Palley, T. I. (2012). A Keynesian theory of hegemonic currencies—Or why the world pays tribute to the dollar. Published at www. thomaspalley. com.

[40] Palley, T. I. (2015). The theory of global imbalances: Mainstream economics vs. structural Keynesianism. Review of Keynesian Economics, 3(1), 45–62. https://doi.org/10.4337/roke.2015.01.04.

The service sector in the United States has grown significantly over time, making the country the world's first "service economy." For example, in 2021, the service sector contributed around 77.6% to GDP.

Figure 1.5 shows the US trade balance broken down into its two main components: the goods balance and the services balance. This figure clearly shows that the US trade imbalance is due to a large deficit in the goods balance and a modest surplus in the services balance.[41] The service sector encompasses a wide range of economic activities that produce services rather than tangible products. The United States has shifted to sectors such as information technology (IT), biotechnology, and financial services, driven by factors such as rising labor costs, technological advances, and the demands of globalization. As the share of the service sector has increased, countries such as the United States have developed significant competitive advantages in global value chains for high-value products such as software development, financial engineering products, and advanced management consulting services.[42] In addition, these countries typically export high-tech, capital-intensive products that generate high value and profit margins in global markets. However, to maintain their economic competitiveness at home, industrialized countries often relocate their labor—and resource-intensive industries to lower-cost developing countries. This geographical redistribution of global production activities helps these countries keep their production costs low and improve the global competitiveness of their companies. However, this strategy also leads to a decline in manufacturing employment and greater dependence on foreign production goods, which affects these countries' trade balance.

Although developed economies are expanding their service sectors, they have been relocating their manufacturing industries, leading to the phenomenon of "industrial hollowing out." This phenomenon not only affects the production capacity of the domestic manufacturing industry

[41] Barattieri, A. (2014). Comparative advantages, trade in services, and global imbalances. Journal of International Economics, 92(1), 1–13. https://doi.org/10.1016/j.jinteco.2013.11.004.

[42] Cova, P., Pisani, M., Batini, N., & Rebucci, A. (2008). Productivity and global imbalances: The role of nontradable total factor productivity in advanced economies. IMF Economic Review. https://doi.org/10.1057/imfsp.2008.5.

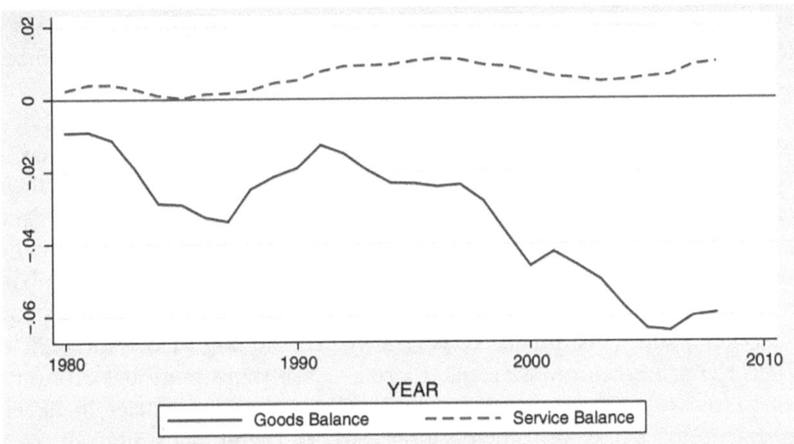

Fig. 1.5 Composition of the US trade balance (as a % of GDP) (*Source* Barattieri, A. (2014). Comparative advantage, service trade, and global imbalances. *Journal of International Economics*, 92(1), 1–13)

but also reinforces the imbalance in the international division of labor.[43] Advanced economies import to compensate for their lack of production capacity, leading to heavy reliance on imported goods. This dependence not only increases the risk of trade deficits but also weakens their economic security. Furthermore, services are less tradable than goods. Indeed, most services are non-tradable and participate in international trade to a much lesser extent than goods. If developed economies make the service sector their leading industry, the advantages of their service sector cannot be reflected in exports, which greatly weakens their export capacity. This low tradability of services not only hinders the speed of development of trade in services but also exacerbates the phenomenon of global trade imbalances. The rise of services has increased the complexity of international economic relations. With the rapid development of the service sector, economic ties and dependencies between countries are growing. However, due to the special nature of the service sector, cooperation and competition between countries in the area of trade in services

[43] Sheng, L., & Nascimento, D. F. D. (2021). Love and Trade War: China and the US in Historical Context. Palgrave Macmillan. doi: https://doi.org/10.1007/978-981-33-4897-4.

have also become more complex and volatile. This complication not only increases the risk of international economic friction but also jeopardizes the stability and development of the global economy.

Conversely, developing countries like China have greatly expanded their manufacturing sectors over the past few decades and created a production structure focused on manufacturing. These countries use their enormous labor resources and relatively low production costs to engage primarily in low-cost production and export to the global market. At the international level, the heavy dependence on exports has led to an unbalanced global economy in which developing countries are dependent on the US market. This imbalance is reflected in the huge US trade deficit. When the US economy weakens, there is a risk that the global economy will follow suit. From textiles to toys to electronics, factories in developing countries have become essential parts of the global supply chain.[44] The example of China is particularly noteworthy, as its rapid industrialization has transformed the country into the "world's factory," exporting mainly labor-intensive goods with low value added. This export-oriented economic model has fueled China's economic growth while accumulating a large trade surplus. However, this model also carries risks associated with dependence on external markets and can lead to an allocation of domestic resources that overly favors export-oriented industries and potentially neglects domestic market development and broader economic diversification. In recent years, China's manufacturing industry has transformed from the "world's factory" into an "intelligent manufacturing powerhouse," and high value-added mechanical and electrical products, such as household appliances, mobile phones, and ships, have taken an important position in the global market. These products not only bring China huge foreign exchange earnings but also promote the optimization and modernization of its industrial structure.

In summary, it can be said that fundamental differences in production structures between services and manufacturing among industrialized and developing countries lead to structural imbalances in global trade. Industrialized countries benefit from trade by exporting high-quality products and services, while developing countries exploit their labor cost advantages in the global market, often facing challenges associated with low

[44] Sheng, L. (2011). Theorising free capital mobility: The perspective of developing countries. Review of International Studies, 37(5), 2519–2534.

value added and low profit margins. While this division of global production and trade increases the efficiency of the global economy to some extent, it also exacerbates international economic inequalities and trade imbalances. Research shows that the richest 1% own 40% of global wealth, the richest 2% own half of global wealth, and the top 10% own 85%; at the other end of the scale, the bottom half of the world's population owns only 1% of global wealth. The Gini coefficient for global adult wealth stands at a staggering 0.89 (or 0.80 in PPP-adjusted estimates).[45]

All indirect signs point to an increase in the concentration of global wealth, which exacerbates global imbalances and inequalities. The Feenstra–Hanson model suggests that low-skilled advanced countries can become skilled. Therefore, the shift of production from industrialized countries to developing countries—through foreign direct investment and import–export trade relations—can lead to greater inequality between the former and the latter.[46] For example, the shift in production through foreign direct investment from the United States to Mexico means that firms that were relatively labor-intensive in the United States are relatively skill-intensive in Mexico (with a higher ratio of skilled to unskilled workers than in domestic firms), increasing relative wages and income inequality in both countries.[47]

The heterogeneity of industrial structures around the world has led to different patterns of economic growth, with a particular distinction between developed and developing countries. Industrialized countries have traditionally relied on a consumption-driven growth model characterized by robust consumer spending, strong demand for imported goods, and the attraction of significant foreign investment in technology—and capital-based industries under conditions of financial liberalization. Consumption-driven economic growth means that consumer demand is ultimately the driving force of economic growth. In developed countries, the share of consumption in GDP is generally higher due to higher per capita income. The increase in consumer demand

[45] Saith, A. (2011). Inequality, imbalance, instability: Reflections on a structural crisis. Development and Change, 42(1), 70–86. https://doi.org/10.1111/j.1467-7660.2011.01705.x.

[46] Feenstra, R. C., & Hanson, G. H. (1995). Foreign investment, outsourcing, and relative wages. https://www.nber.org/papers/w5121.

[47] Zhu, S. C., & Trefler, D. (2001). Ginis in general equilibrium: Trade, technology, and inequality in the South. https://www.nber.org/papers/w8446.

leads to an increase in economic activities such as production, investment, and employment, thereby promoting economic growth. Specifically, the mechanism of consumption-driven economic growth includes the following aspects:

(1) **Demand-pull effect:** The increase in consumer demand will directly drive the development of related industries, such as services and manufacturing. The development of these industries will further drive employment and investment, thus forming a virtuous cycle of economic growth.
(2) **Investment guidance effect:** The increase in consumer demand will encourage enterprises to increase their investments to meet market demand. These investments not only help improve the production efficiency of enterprises but also drive the development of related industrial chains and promote economic growth.
(3) **Technological innovation effect:** The upgrading of consumer demand will encourage enterprises to carry out technological innovations and product upgrades to meet market demand. These technological innovations and product upgrades not only enhance the competitiveness of enterprises but also promote the progress and development of the entire industry. From the perspective of the economic development process of developed countries, the model of consumption-driven economic growth has achieved remarkable results.

In the United States, for example, consumer spending has become an important component of GDP and contributes much more to economic growth than investment and exports. Furthermore, with the deepening of globalization, the model of consumption-driven economic growth has been gradually promoted and adopted in other industrialized countries. Despite the remarkable successes of the consumption-driven economic growth model, there are also potential risks. First, excessive reliance on consumption can lead to economic overheating and the formation of bubbles, which increases economic risks. Second, fluctuations in consumer demand have a direct impact on the stability of economic growth and lead to economic fluctuations and cyclical adjustments.

The US economy grew at its fastest pace since 1984 in 2021, recovering from the recession caused by the COVID-19 pandemic. According to the US Bureau of Economic Analysis (BEA), real GDP grew by 5.7% in 2021, more than offsetting the 3.4% decline in the previous year. However, the rise in private consumer spending (on both goods and services) and private domestic investment were the main drivers of this recovery, as government spending stagnated and imports exceeded exports, resulting in an overall negative contribution from international trade.[48] This consumption-driven model is not unique to the United States but widespread in many industrialized countries, where domestic markets are heavily supported by a steady flow of imported goods and services, further increasing global dependence on trade relations. Similar trends can be observed in Europe, where economic growth is often supported by consumer spending and investment in high-tech and capital-intensive industries. This model promotes a cycle of economic activity in which high consumer spending drives demand for continued imports of goods while attracting foreign direct investment into the market. However, economic theory predicts that trade deficits will displace employment from domestic goods-producing sectors, which is a widely held view in political circles.[49] The trade deficits created by this borrowing have played an important role in the decline of the US economy.[50]

Between 1992 and 2012, the NFA of the United States deteriorated by $4 trillion as US households and the government borrowed from the rest of the world. Over the same period, the share of the goods sector in total employment declined sharply. The dependence of industrialized countries on a consumption-driven economic growth model puts enormous pressure on global resources. As consumer demand rises, so does resource consumption. The manufacturing of consumer goods requires large amounts of energy, raw materials, and water resources, which places a huge burden on the environment. At the same time, the increase in waste poses a threat to the ecosystem. As consumer demand for consumer goods such as fast fashion and electronics increases, product

48 World Economic Forum. (2022, February 1). Consumer spending and private investment drive US GDP growth. https://www.weforum.org/agenda/2022/02/consumer-spending-private-investment-drive-gdp-growth/.

49 Kehoe, T. J., Ruhl, K. J., & Steinberg, J. B. (2018). Global imbalances and structural change in the United States. Journal of Political Economy, 126(2), 761–796.

50 Scott, R. E. (2015). Manufacturing job losses: Trade, not productivity, is the culprit. Economic Policy Institute Working Paper 402.

life cycles are shortening and the problem of resource waste and environmental pollution is becoming increasingly serious. To achieve sustainable development, industrialized countries must increase their investments in green technologies and sustainable products to promote the development of a circular economy. However, such a transition may require time and resources, and the impact on global imbalances also needs to be monitored. In addition, fluctuations in consumer demand in industrialized countries can lead to global economic fluctuations. When consumer demand in industrialized countries declines, global growth can suffer. The dependence of industrialized countries on a consumption-driven economic growth model can lead to global investment imbalances. Due to the attractiveness of consumer markets in industrialized countries, large amounts of capital can flow into these countries, leading to the capital shortage problem in developing countries.[51] Such investment imbalances not only hamper economic growth in developing countries but can also exacerbate global imbalances. At the same time, excessive capital flows to industrialized countries can lead to asset bubbles and financial risks.

In contrast, developing countries have historically relied primarily on foreign investment and exports as drivers of economic growth, focusing on expanding their production capacity and improving efficiency to increase export volumes. According to David Ricardo's theory of comparative advantage, developing countries generally have relatively large labor forces and therefore have comparative advantages in labor-intensive industries. By exporting labor-intensive products such as textiles, clothing, and toys, these countries can earn foreign exchange and boost economic growth. In addition, the Heckscher–Ohlin model explains how developing countries use their abundant factors—whether unskilled labor or natural resources—to specialize in the corresponding export sectors. Export activity provides developing countries with valuable foreign exchange earnings, which can be used to import advanced technologies, equipment, and raw materials, thereby improving the competitiveness of domestic industries. At the same time, foreign exchange earnings can be used to repay foreign debt, stabilize the exchange rate, and maintain the balance of payments, thereby creating a stable external environment for economic development. In addition, increased export earnings can promote capital accumulation and create a material basis for economic

[51] Sheng, L. (2016). Explaining economic imbalances between the US and China: A social perspective. Cambridge Review of International Affairs, 29(3), 1097–1111.

growth. This strategy has proven very effective: from 1990 to 2017, the share of developing countries in global exports rose from 16 to 30%.[52] This expansion has been instrumental in integrating these economies into the global market and promoting economic development and poverty reduction.

A lack of capital is an obstacle to the expansion of production and investment in developing countries. As a result, developing countries have high per capita savings rates among countries, companies, and individuals. High savings rates provide developing countries with a sufficient source of capital accumulation, which is an important foundation for economic growth. In developing countries, the lack of capital is often one of the main obstacles to economic growth. A high savings rate means that more funds can be used for investments such as infrastructure construction, industrial modernization, and technological innovation. These investment activities can not only directly improve production capacity and efficiency but also promote the development of related industries through spillover effects, thus forming a positive cycle of economic growth.

At the international level, by increasing domestic savings and capital accumulation, developing countries can rely more on their own strengths in technological research and development (R&D) and industrial modernization and reduce their dependence on external technologies and markets. A high savings rate also means more foreign exchange reserves, which helps to stabilize the exchange rate and improve the sustainability of the balance of payments, thereby achieving more competitive advantages in the international market. High savings rates also facilitate the development and deepening of financial markets. When savings rise, financial institutions have access to more sources of financing, can increase the volume of credit, and improve the range and quality of financial services.

At the same time, a high savings rate promotes innovation and diversification of financial products, meets the needs of different investors, and promotes the prosperity and stability of the financial market. A high savings rate also contributes to social stability and security. In developing countries, people tend to save more than they spend due to economic fluctuations and social risks. A high savings rate means that people

[52] World Bank. (2023, February 12). Trade is a powerful engine for economic development and poverty reduction. https://www.worldbank.org/en/topic/trade/brief/trade-has-been-a-powerful-driver-of-economic-development-and-poverty-reduction.

have more financial reserves and are better able to cope with emergencies and uncertainties, thus reducing social risks and uncertainties. This stability and sense of security help to strengthen consumer confidence and their willingness to invest, further stimulating economic development. However, high savings rates also have a number of negative consequences for developing countries. They can lead to insufficient consumption and weak domestic demand, even though consumption is one of the most important drivers of economic growth in developing countries.

However, if the savings rate is too high, residents tend to save their income rather than spend it, leading to insufficient domestic demand and a lack of sustainable impetus for economic growth. This lack of consumption could also lead to problems such as overcapacity and higher unemployment, further hampering economic growth. A high savings rate can lead to an imbalance in the investment structure. In developing countries, high savings rates can lead to overinvestment and inefficient investment due to problems such as imperfect market mechanisms and asymmetric information. Some industries or sectors may suffer from overcapacity and cut-throat competition due to overinvestment, while others may lag behind due to insufficient resources. This structural imbalance in investment not only wastes resources but can also trigger economic fluctuations and risks. High savings rates can also increase risks in financial markets. In developing countries, high savings rates can lead to excessive wealth and financial market bubbles due to problems such as underdeveloped financial markets and imperfect regulatory mechanisms. When savings flow into financial markets, asset prices can rise and asset bubbles can form. Once the bubble bursts, it causes turmoil and risks in the financial market, which affect economic development. Furthermore, while high savings rates lead to larger foreign exchange reserves and greater international competitiveness, they can also increase developing countries' dependence on external markets and resources. Fluctuations in the external market or problems with the supply of resources have serious implications for the economic development of developing countries. This external dependence and vulnerability increase the uncertainty and risk of economic development as a whole.

The financial systems of many developing countries, which are primarily bank-centric and have less developed capital markets, pose significant barriers to small and medium-sized enterprises (SMEs) seeking external financing. These financial structures often lack the diversity and maturity to offer the whole range of financing options typically available in developed markets, which can slow down entrepreneurial activity and innovation. SMEs in these regions often face higher borrowing costs and stricter collateral requirements, which can hamper their growth and ability to compete nationally and internationally. In reality, global cross-border capital flows have reached unprecedented levels, but only a fraction has been directed to developing countries. More than a decade ago, Lucas pointed out the weakness of the standard neoclassical growth model that explains the behavior of international capital flows.[53] These models predict that countries with a lower ratio of capital to labor should have higher marginal returns, so international capital should flow from rich to poor countries. However, in Lucas's terminology, capital began to flow from poor to rich countries, or "upstream." The need for these companies to finance themselves through the accumulation of savings therefore highlights another challenge: high savings can lead to capital being tied up in unproductive uses, exacerbating the problems associated with high savings, capital illiquidity, and the export-oriented growth model that prevails in these countries. This situation often leads to misallocation of resources, with funds that could be used to expand business activities or invest in new technologies being held in reserve. This tendency toward high savings among companies in developing countries not only reflects inefficiencies in the financial sector but also contributes to general macroeconomic imbalances, which are reflected, for example, in current account surpluses or deficits.[54]

Furthermore, the export-oriented growth model, while offering numerous advantages, exposes these economies to global market fluctuations. Dependence on foreign markets for economic stability can be risky, especially in scenarios where global demand slows or international trade policy takes an unfavorable turn. This growth pattern has led to imbalances in global trade. International trade relations involve complex elements and asymmetries that are often reflected in bilateral trade imbalances, which affect countries' external positions and consequently lead

[53] Lucas, R. (1990). Why doesn't capital flow from rich to poor countries? American Economic Review, 80(2), 92–6.

[54] Tan, Z., Yao, Y., & Wei, S. J. (2015). Financial structure, corporate savings and current account imbalances. Journal of International Money and Finance, 54, 142–167. https://doi.org/10.1016/j.jimonfin.2015.02.012.

to distortions and a potential increase in protectionist pressures.[55] Trade imbalances are associated with economic crises and instability: the fact that large imbalances imply large capital inflows can lead to instability in importing countries. Due to the link with the current account, trade surpluses are typically associated with high investment and high savings in countries. For example, countries with low incomes and high expected returns can borrow abroad to finance their development.[56] However, recent developments in international capital markets make it possible to invest in any country (not just domestically). Thus, if a country saves more than it invests, this surplus can be absorbed by international capital markets, leading to a "savings glut."[57]

In summary, it can be said that these contrasting growth models contribute to persistent global imbalances. Industrialized countries rely on consumption, while developing countries rely on foreign investment and exports. While different growth strategies have improved some aspects of global economic efficiency to some extent, they have also exacerbated international economic inequality, reinforced economic disparities between industrialized and developing countries, and led to persistent trade imbalances and an unequal distribution of global economic power and wealth. China and other surplus countries cannot rely indefinitely on excessive foreign consumption to support their export expansion and production growth, while deficit countries also face problems because their trade and current account deficits are due to excessive reliance on foreign borrowing to support consumption and growth.[58] The most important empirical fact is that trade imbalances persist. It is worth noting that most of the trade imbalances that have emerged recently are primarily attributable to the trade imbalance between the United States

[55] Bracke, T., Bussière, M., Fidora, M., & Straub, R. (2010). A framework for assessing global imbalances 1. The World Economy, 33(9), 1140–1174. https://doi.org/10.1111/j.1467-9701.2010.01266.x.

[56] Krugman, P. R. (2009). International Economics: Theory and Policy. Prentice Hall.

[57] Bernanke, B. S. (2005). The global saving glut and the US current account deficit: A speech at the Sandridge Lecture, Virginia Association of Economics, Richmond, Virginia, March 10, 2005 and the Homer Jones Lecture, St. Louis, Missouri, on April 14, 2005. Speech by the Board of Governors of the Federal Reserve System (US).

[58] Sheng, L. (2014). Economic structure, cost outsourcing, and global imbalances. Journal of Australian Political Economy, 74, 81–94.

and China, which is actually one of the most structurally unbalanced bilateral relationships in the current international trade network.[59]

The production structures and growth patterns of different countries may also influence each other, which could further exacerbate existing global imbalances. If industrialized countries encounter obstacles to the development of their high-end industries—due to factors such as technological stagnation, market saturation, or regulatory challenges—their ability to maintain their dominance in global markets could decline. If developing countries simultaneously improve their industrial capabilities rapidly, perhaps through technological leaps, increased foreign investment, or significant improvements in labor productivity, traditional trade patterns could change significantly. This shifting landscape could disrupt traditional trade patterns, in which developed countries export high-value technological goods while developing countries focus on manufacturing low-end goods. This could lead to an uneven distribution of resources between different countries and industries, as well as to changes in the structure of employment.

As developing countries move up the value chain, they begin to compete directly with industrialized countries, which may lead to a redistribution of economic activities that may not follow historical patterns. This new competitive environment could result in an allocation of resources that favors emerging industrial centers in developing countries and forces traditional powers to adapt. Furthermore, such changes in global production and trade dynamics could lead to significant changes in global labor markets.

In industrialized countries, workers could shift from manufacturing to the service sector or to new industries requiring different skills, exacerbating problems such as unemployment or underemployment due to skills gaps. In developing countries, rapid industrial modernization could lead to a sharp increase in demand for highly skilled workers. This could alter wage structures and employment patterns and potentially lead to social upheaval if the changes are too abrupt or not accompanied by appropriate social policies. These interactions between different national production structures and growth models can therefore not only exacerbate existing global imbalances but also create complex challenges for international

59 Serrano, M. Á., Boguñá, M., & Vespignani, A. (2007). Patterns of dominant trade flows in the world trade network. Journal of Economic Interaction and Coordination, 2(2), 111–124. https://doi.org/10.1007/s11403-007-0026-y.

trade, resource distribution, and labor market stability that require coordinated policy responses to mitigate negative effects and increase economic resilience.

1.3 The Impact of Cost Outsourcing on Global Imbalances

We live in the age of outsourcing. Companies appear to be outsourcing more and more activities to subcontractors, from product design to assembly, from R&D to marketing, sales, and customer service. Some companies have even gone so far as to become "virtual" manufacturers, owning the designs for many products but manufacturing almost nothing themselves.[60] In today's global economy, outsourcing plays a key role in business operations, providing companies with cost-effective solutions and access to expertise. Recent statistics show how widespread outsourcing is and what its impact is. According to Statista, the global outsourcing market was estimated at $92.5 billion in 2021 and is expected to grow at a rate of 5.84% from 2022 to 2028. According to a report by Deloitte, 59% of companies outsource to save costs and 57% to focus on their core functions. These figures highlight the important role outsourcing plays in modern business strategy by increasing efficiency and enabling companies to remain competitive in a rapidly changing environment. A closer look at outsourcing statistics reveals that outsourcing has a cross-industry and cross-regional impact, shaping the way companies operate and thrive in today's connected world. In the context of economic globalization, companies distribute their production factors globally and implement a refined industrial division of labor through the new form of offshore outsourcing, which has an impact on both their own production efficiency and on the wage levels of companies.[61]

Traditionally, outsourcing is understood as the "use of external resources," i.e., the creation of value outside rather than inside a company.

[60] Helfer, S. (1991). Strategy and irreversibility in supplier relationships: The case of the US automotive industry. Business History Review, 65(4), 781–824. https://doi.org/10.2307/3117265.

[61] Geishecker, I., & Goerg, H. (2008). Winners and losers: A micro-level analysis of international outsourcing and wages. Canadian Journal of Economics, 41(1), 243–270. https://doi.org/10.1111/j.1365-2966.2008.00462.x.

From this perspective, the boundaries of a company become more interesting, because it raises the strategic question of how external resources can be used effectively. Above all, it is not enough to simply acknowledge the existence of external resources. External resources must be used by and for companies to strengthen their position in the face of competition.[62] Outsourcing costs has become an aggressive decision for companies to continuously promote the optimal allocation of resources, divest non-core businesses, and emphasize the competitiveness of their core businesses, resulting in the flow of production factors such as labor and raw materials between different countries and regions. Outsourcing has become a big business and its effective management is critical to the future success of a company.[63] The widespread use of such resource flows has significantly altered the industrial structures and economic operating models of many countries. This change often disrupts the original economic balance by relocating industries, redistributing labor, and redefining global trade patterns.

With the increasing fragmentation and globalization of production, the original role of countries in the global value chain is changing, further exacerbating existing global imbalances and creating new economic dependencies that affect both developed and developing economies. This process of cost outsourcing is not only about reducing operating costs but also about improving a company's agility and ability to compete in an increasingly interconnected global market. By shifting labor-intensive activities with low value added to countries with cheap labor, companies can focus their domestic resources on high-value tasks such as R&D, marketing, and innovation. This reallocation of resources enables companies to strengthen their position in the competitive global economy, but it also raises concerns about labor markets, wage disparities, and job losses in countries where outsourcing is most widespread.[64] Therefore,

[62] Arnold, U. (2000). New dimensions of outsourcing: A combination of transaction cost economics and the concept of core competencies. European Journal of Purchasing & Supply Management, 6(1), 23–29. https://doi.org/10.1016/S0969-7012(99)00028-3.

[63] Kakabadse, A. (2001). Smart Sourcing: International best practice. Springer.

[64] Sheng, L. (2016). Explaining US-China economic imbalances: A social perspective. Cambridge Review of International Affairs, 29, 1097–1111. https://dx.doi.org/10.1080/09557571.2016.1230589.

outsourcing has a profound impact on the microeconomic level of individual companies and on the macroeconomic level of countries around the world.

The conclusion regarding the advantages of outsourcing and the gains from trade has been questioned by Gomory and Baumol (2000) and Samuelson (2004). These authors use pure trade theory to examine the question of the international catching-up process and conclude that a country can lose if the catching-up process takes place in the export industry of the advanced country. In this case, the advanced country experiences an adverse terms of trade effect because the global supply of its export products increases.[65] This cost-cutting initiative brings a number of advantages to industrialized countries. By reducing production costs, companies are able to improve the competitiveness of their products in the international market, enabling them to sell their goods at lower prices without losing their profit margins. Outsourcing is the result of intensive efforts by TNKs based in the North to reduce their costs and increase their profits by replacing domestic workers with higher wages with low-wage workers from the South.[66] Stephen Roach (2003, pp. 5–6), a senior economist at Morgan Stanley, calls this phenomenon "global labor arbitrage" and argues that the "relentless search for new efficiency gains, by extracting products from relatively low-paid workers in developing countries has become an increasingly urgent survival tactic for companies in developed economies." This benefits not only companies but also consumers, as lower production costs lead to more affordable goods and greater choice. The influx of cheap imported goods improves consumer welfare by increasing their purchasing power and making a greater variety of products available to consumers of all income levels.

In addition to cost reductions and consumer benefits, outsourcing enables companies to focus on core competencies such as R&D, innovation, and high-quality services. By outsourcing routine production tasks, companies in industrialized countries can allocate more resources to activities requiring advanced skills and technologies, further fueling economic

[65] Palley, T. (2008). The economics of outsourcing: How should policy respond? Review of Social Economy, 66(3), 279–295. https://doi.org/10.1080/003467607018 21896.

[66] Smith, J. (2012). Outsourcing, financialization, and the crisis. International Journal of Management Concepts and Philosophy, 6(1–2), 19–44. https://doi.org/10.1504/ IJMCP.2012.047205.

growth in sectors such as finance, healthcare, and technology. Companies are outsourcing activities they consider non-core to their business and focusing on their "core" activities, leading many to become more specialized while pursuing other value-added goals.[67] This restructuring also encourages companies to rethink and rescale their production processes, improving overall production efficiency and creating new business models that could take advantage of global supply chains. However, the rapid shift of production steps and jobs to low-wage countries also has a significant impact on labor markets in industrialized countries. The outsourcing of manufacturing jobs is displacing many workers in industries such as textiles, electronics, and automobiles, leading to rising unemployment and wage stagnation in some sectors. This shift also contributes to growing income inequality, as the benefits of outsourcing accrue primarily to companies and consumers, while displaced workers struggle to adapt to new economic realities. Governments in industrialized countries have had to address these challenges and have often introduced retraining programs and protectionist measures to mitigate the social and economic consequences of widespread outsourcing. In addition, some studies highlight the risks associated with outsourcing. For example, Earl discusses 11 risks associated with IT outsourcing: the possibility of weak management, inexperienced employees, business uncertainty, outdated technological knowledge, endemic uncertainty, hidden costs, lack of organizational learning, loss of innovation capacity, the dangers associated with a perpetual triangle, indivisibility of technology, and blurred focus.[68]

Between the 1960s and 1980s, the share of manufacturing in GDP in the United States declined significantly, from 28 to 21%. This decline represented a significant shift in the economic structure of the United States and reflected broader changes in industrial priorities and economic

[67] Willman, J. (1999, September 22). Unilever focuses on key "power brands." Financial Times, p. 25.

[68] Earl, M. J. (1996). The risks of outsourcing IT. MIT Sloan Management Review. Research Feature Spring 1996.

focus. In 2007, this downward trend continued, with the share of manufacturing in GDP falling further to just 12%.[69,70] In contrast, countries such as Singapore, Taiwan, South Korea, and China experienced rapid and profound growth in their manufacturing sectors during this period. These countries have not only expanded their industrial capacities but also become important players in global outsourcing networks, particularly in relation to the United States. China's rise to become the world's leading manufacturing country in 2011 represents a significant milestone in the global economic arena. This success underscores China's growing influence and its expanding role in international trade and manufacturing. After becoming the world's second largest economy, China has emerged as a major economic powerhouse that is reshaping global economic dynamics and underscoring its growing influence on the world stage.

Confident in the labor cost advantage offered by the demographic dividend, the manufacturing sector in developing countries is engaging in processing, production, assembly, and other manufacturing activities and is rapidly integrating into the global division of labor in the value chain. This integration brings a significant number of employment opportunities and a considerable boost to economic growth. However, the creation of a large number of low-end manufacturing industries has also brought a number of challenges to these countries, including excessive resource consumption and environmental pollution. Developing countries may have achieved rapid economic growth in the short term, but if they fail to modernize their industries and innovate technologically in the long term, this may lead them to rely on low value-added industries and to relocate manufacturing to other countries due to low costs. This could lead to a pattern of contraction and limited growth potential. Although some high-tech products are manufactured in developing countries and then exported, the majority of integrated high-tech inputs come from

[69] Pierce, J. R., & Schott, P. K. (2016). The surprisingly rapid decline in US manufacturing employment. American Economic Review, 106(7), 1632–1662.

[70] Botta, A. (2010). Economic development, structural change, and booms in natural resources: a structuralist perspective. Metroeconomica, 61(3), 510–539. https://doi.org/10.1111/j.1467-999X.2009.04077.x.

industrialized countries.[71] As a result, trade advantages are concentrated in industrialized countries.[72]

Take China as an example. Although the international organization of TNC production to some extent promotes the technological modernization of the Chinese manufacturing industry through foreign direct investment and outsourcing via the physical capital channel, the impact on the human capital and R&D capital channel is generally negative. In particular, outsourcing the organization of production can effectively control the diffusion and spillover of technology and skills. This reinforces the low-skilled labor model and is the main cause of micro-production organization for the path dependence on technological modernization and skill upgrading in China's manufacturing industry.[73]

In industrialized countries, the practice of cost outsourcing has led to the relocation of some traditional manufacturing industries, resulting in a decline in domestic employment opportunities, particularly in the lower and middle-tier manufacturing sectors. This has not only affected the stability of the labor market but also undermined the foundations of the domestic manufacturing sector, which in turn affects the innovative capacity and competitiveness of the economy as a whole.[74] At the same time, extensive use of cost outsourcing can lead to technological spillovers, enabling developing countries to advance more rapidly in related industries, thus further exacerbating imbalances in the global economy. Cost outsourcing leads to imbalances in international trade. The country where the outsourcing company is located usually has a trade deficit, while the outsourcing country has a trade surplus. If this trade

[71] Baldwin, R. (2016). The Great Convergence: Information Technology and the New Globalization. The Belknap Press of Harvard University.

[72] Amiti, M., & Wei, S. J. (2005). Offshoring of services, production, and employment: Evidence from the United States. IMF working paper no. 05238.

[73] Hong L.Y., Han F., & Tang Y. (2016). Why is it difficult for China's manufacturing industry to break through the technical and skill upgrade trap? An analysis from the perspective of international production organization arrangements. (Zhong guo zhi zao ye wei he nan yi tu po ji shu ji neng sheng ji xian jing?--yi ge guo ji sheng chan zu zhi an pai shi jiao de fen xi). Quantitative Economic and Technological Economic Research, 3, 23–40.

[74] Acemoglu, D., Author, D., Dorn, D., Hanson, G., & Price, B. (2014). The return of the Solow paradox? IT, productivity, and employment in U.S. manufacturing. American Economic Review, 104(5), 394–399._https://www.aeaweb.org/articles?id=10.1257/aer.104.5.394.

imbalance is not addressed effectively in the long term, it can lead to trade conflicts and protectionism, thereby undermining the stability and balance of the global economy.

The trade war between the United States and China in 2018 is a prime example of how outsourcing practices and persistent trade deficits have led to significant economic imbalances. The United States was eager to address its trade deficit with China, which had been exacerbated by the massive outsourcing of manufacturing jobs to China. The tariffs imposed by the United States were aimed at reducing its trade deficit and promoting domestic production. However, they also led to retaliatory tariffs from China, which disrupted global supply chains and increased costs for American consumers and businesses. This conflict is an example of how unresolved trade imbalances and outsourcing practices can escalate into broader economic disputes that destabilize global trade and adversely affect economic relations on a large scale. Outsourcing also contributes to the "financialization" of global imbalances. The direct and indirect effects of large-scale outsourcing of production processes to low-wage countries contribute to the low interest rates, low inflation, and low volatility that characterize the so-called "Goldilocks" economy.[75] The inflationary pressure generated by credit-financed demand expansion is being significantly mitigated by falling prices for outsourced inputs and consumer goods, while China and other manufacturing exporters keep interest rates and volatility low by returning export earnings to the US government in the form of loans at zero or negative real interest rates. The "global imbalances" that fuel financialization are thus essentially the result of the shift of production abroad. Just as low interest rates encourage consumers and businesses to take on more debt, they also force banks to become increasingly desperate for "yield" by investing savers' money in risky financial assets.

Although cost outsourcing has greatly facilitated global factor mobility, it has also contributed to the exacerbation of global economic imbalances in several ways. Outsourcing leads to fragmentation of international production, and some researchers examine the possible relationship between trade imbalances and fragmentation of international production

[75] Smith, J. (2012). Outsourcing, financialisation and the crisis. International Journal of Management Concepts and Philosophy, 6(1–2), 19–44. https://doi.org/10.1504/IJMCP.2012.047205.

using empirical methods. Their results show that international fragmentation of production is, on average, positively and significantly associated with countries' trade balances.[76] Further research shows that the trade balance deteriorates as offshoring to countries with lower income/lower product quality increases, and improves as offshoring to countries with higher income/higher product quality increases. In particular, international fragmentation of production increases both exports and imports, but the positive net effect occurs when offshoring takes place to countries with higher income/higher product quality.[77]

These imbalances can deepen social divisions and intensify competition for resources, potentially undermining the very stability that economic cooperation is intended to promote. Outsourcing should be viewed as a qualitative phenomenon that is best understood as a new form of competition. In response, policy measures must be developed to strengthen national competitiveness and establish new rules governing the nature of global competition.[78] To achieve the sustainable and balanced development of the global economy, countries must seize the opportunities offered by cost outsourcing, such as increased efficiency and access to new markets, while addressing the associated challenges. This includes developing policies that support local industries and workers affected by outsourcing, promote fair trade practices, and strengthen corporate social responsibility. There is also a need to support job losses and active labor market policies that help laid-off workers cope with income losses and receive training for productive employment in the future. In addition, concerted efforts must be made to rebalance the global economy by promoting innovation, investing in education and infrastructure, and creating an environment that supports equitable growth and opportunity for all nations. With this multifaceted approach, the global community can work toward an economic landscape that is not only more efficient but also more equitable and resilient.

[76] Gu, X.H. and Sheng. L. (2010). A sensible tool for Pareto-Improvement: Capital Controls. Journal of World Trade, 44(3), 567–590.

[77] Felice, G., & Tajoli, L. (2021). Trade balances and global value chains: Is there a link? Structural Change and Economic Dynamics, 59, 228–246. https://doi.org/10.1016/j.strueco.2021.08.013.

[78] Palley, T. (2008). The economics of outsourcing: How should policy respond? Review of Social Economy, 66(3), 279–295. https://doi.org/10.1080/00346760701821896.

1.4 The Impact of Globalization on Global Imbalances

Since the 1980s, the global economy has become increasingly "networked" and "integrated." On the one hand, falling transport costs and the spread of information and communication technologies mean that the concept of "distance" has rapidly lost its meaning; on the other hand, gross trade, foreign direct investment, capital flows, and technology transfer have increased significantly.[79] Globalization is a major trend in current global economic development, characterized by the deepening of economic relations between countries and the integration of the world economy through trade and capital flows.[80] This integration has led to greater interdependence between economies, which encourages economic exchanges and investments across borders. However, global imbalances and financial instability are closely intertwined and can be attributed to a common cause: financial globalization within the current monetary and financial system. Financial globalization has exacerbated these imbalances by hindering effective exchange rate adjustments, promoting export-oriented growth strategies, and perpetuating persistent financial deficits.[81] Furthermore, this process has led to an unequal distribution of economic benefits and a significant increase in economic inequality between countries. The resulting economic inequalities highlight the difficulty of ensuring that the benefits of global economic integration are distributed fairly among all nations. Pessimists point out that globalization has very uneven effects and leads to negative spillover effects on previously protected sectors, the marginalization of entire regions from the global economy, and a possible increase in income inequality within countries.[82] With the rapid development of global economic integration,

[79] Lee, E., & Vivarelli, M. (2006). The social impact of globalization in developing countries. International Labor Review., 145, 167. https://doi.org/10.1111/j.1564-913X.2006.tb00016.x.

[80] O'Rourke, K. H., & Williamson, J. G. (1999). Globalization and History: The Evolution of a Nineteenth-Century Atlantic Economy. MIT Press.

[81] Liang, Y. (2012). Global imbalances and financial crisis: Financial globalization as a common cause. Journal of Economic Issues, 46(2), 353–362. https://doi.org/10.2753/JEI0021-3624460210.

[82] Lee, E., & Vivarelli, M. (2006). The social impact of globalization in developing countries. International Labor Review, 145, 167. https://doi.org/10.1111/j.1564-913X.2006.tb00016.x.

financial globalization has shown unbalanced and incomplete characteristics. Financial market imperfections can affect the direction of net capital flows and the corresponding composition of gross capital flows through various channels. For example, regional financial inadequacies can lead to a global undersupply of "safe" assets and trigger net capital flows to regions that produce safe assets. Financial inadequacies can also lead to differences in relative domestic savings patterns between economies with low levels of financial development and those with well-functioning and deep financial markets, which are attributable to differences in the ability to insure against future risks.[83]

A well-developed and well-functioning financial system leads to a deepening of financial markets, which reduces domestic savings. First, countries with more developed financial markets tend to save less and accumulate net foreign debt. Conversely, countries with imperfect and more volatile financial markets may have higher savings (e.g., due to a lack of insurance), but also greater capital outflows (due to the desire to seek safer returns). Second, differences between financial markets also affect the composition of international portfolios. Countries with better financial markets can invest in higher-yielding assets. They therefore receive payments even if their net foreign position is negative. In such an environment, low-income countries with low levels of financial development would be worse off, as their savings could bypass the domestic financial sector and flow, at least in the short term, to developed countries with highly developed financial markets. Financial deficiencies therefore increase savings and the demand for assets.

From a trade policy perspective, globalization has profoundly changed the structure of international economic interactions and led to a much more complex and sophisticated division of labor between countries. According to the theory of relative comparative advantage, both trade and foreign direct investment should benefit from the abundance of labor in developing countries, triggering a trend toward specialization in labor-intensive activities at home and thus expanding local employment. As companies in different countries increasingly seek to optimize their production processes and tap into larger global markets, this quest has

83 Bracke, T., Bussière, M., Fidora, M., & Straub, R. (2010). A framework for assessing global imbalances 1. Die Weltwirtschaft, 33(9), 1140–1174. https://doi.org/10.1111/j.1467-9701.2010.01266.x.

triggered a significant trend toward the transnational relocation of industries. This movement is driven by the desire to find and use lower-cost factors of production and to exploit economies of scale on a global scale. In this context, developing countries have abundant and relatively cheap labor resources, making them extremely attractive locations for the relocation of labor-intensive industries such as textiles, electronics assembly, and various manufacturing processes. This influx of industries has not only boosted economic growth in these developing countries but also led to a remarkable increase in their export volumes, enabling them to accumulate trade surpluses over time. These surpluses are a direct result of their competitive advantage in producing goods at lower cost, which in turn increases their export capacity. Conversely, developed countries with advanced technologies and extensive capital resources have shifted their focus to high value-added industries and services.[84] They have specialized in manufacturing and exporting high-end products such as cutting-edge technology, sophisticated machinery, and premium services.

Although this strategy has enabled them to gain a competitive advantage and generate substantial profits, it has also contributed to trade imbalances. Industrialized countries often have trade deficits in labor-intensive sectors, while recording surpluses in high-tech and service-oriented areas. This imbalance reflects the different economic structures and competitive advantages that characterize the global market landscape. The resulting imbalances highlight the complex dynamics of global trade and underscore the challenges associated with achieving balanced economic growth across different regions. The theory of unbalanced growth, first proposed by Professor Hirschman, views development as a series of unbalanced chain reactions. This theory suggests that due to differences in resource endowments and levels of economic development between different regions, their geographical advantages vary. Therefore, it is necessary to determine a focus and main direction of investment when allocating resources and to invest resources in a planned manner in advantageous regions or industries so that they form "development poles" to drive the joint development of surrounding regions and industries. This unbalanced growth pattern can lead some regions or industries to develop rapidly while others lag behind, exacerbating global imbalances.

[84] Rodrik, D. (2011). The globalization paradox: Democracy and the future of the world economy. World Trade Review, 10(1), 409–417. https://doi.org/10.1017/S1474745611000231.

Furthermore, research suggests that globalization and free trade may erode rich countries and make trade even more unbalanced. In 2004, the Nobel Prize winner Paul Samuelson published an article pointing out that, under certain circumstances, free trade can erode the comparative advantage of rich countries and make them worse off.[85] He presents a theoretical model with two countries (one with high wages and one with low wages) and two goods (one with high value added and one with low value added). He shows that the terms of trade of the industrialized country deteriorate dramatically if the low-wage country has a large number of workers capable of producing the high value-added good and if its relative productivity in this good increases, leaving the industrialized country worse off.

In terms of capital flows, globalization has fundamentally changed the landscape of international finance, prompting global capital to actively seek higher returns across borders. However, in the current international monetary and financial system, this flow of capital has led to a misguided credit boom, increased the accumulation of financial risks, and further exacerbated global imbalances. The fundamental weaknesses of the international monetary and financial system can be attributed to the problem of "excessive elasticity": the system lacks sufficiently strong anchors to prevent the accumulation of unsustainable booms in credit and asset prices (financial imbalances), which can ultimately lead to severe financial tensions and derail the global economy.[86]

"Elasticity" is defined as the extent to which monetary and financial institutions restrict the process of credit creation and the availability of debt capital in general. Low restriction implies high elasticity. Reducing this elasticity requires anchoring in financial and monetary systems and prudent fiscal policy. However, the current international monetary system has no clear anchor point. The monetary policy of the United States has a global impact. When the United States lowers interest rates, it encourages American capital to invest abroad. Other countries under pressure from rising exchange rates will decide to lower interest rates while increasing their foreign exchange reserves. Lower interest rates attract

85 Ricardo, W., & Rebut, M. (2004). Confirm the arguments of mainstream economists who support globalization. Journal of Economic Perspectives, 18(3), 135–146.

86 Borio, C., & Disyatat, P. (2010). Global imbalances and the financial crisis: A reassessment of the role of international financial markets. Asian Economic Policy Review, 5(2), 198–216. https://doi.org/10.1111/j.1748-3131.2010.01163.x.

large inflows of foreign investment. The global economy is developing at two speeds. On the one hand, advanced industrialized countries, which have been hardest hit by the crisis, are experiencing weak growth and economic weakness. On the other hand, emerging economies, particularly in Asia, are experiencing strong growth after a brief slowdown. Differing growth prospects and very low interest rates in core countries have created upward pressure on exchange rates in emerging economies, triggering large capital inflows and supporting a sharp rise in credit and asset prices in these countries. This has increased the risk of financial imbalances building up, not unlike what happened in the years leading up to the 1997 Asian crisis.[87]

Capital flows have led to a significant inflow of capital from developed to developing countries, contributing significantly to stronger economic growth and improved export capacity in these emerging economies. When regions and industries experience accelerated economic growth, they naturally attract not only significant amounts of financial capital but also human capital and advanced technologies that further stimulate their development and innovation. This influx of investment often puts pressure on local currencies, leading to potential appreciation that can hamper export competitiveness. It also raises concerns about the risk of asset bubbles in countries and regions with underdeveloped financial systems and regulatory frameworks. These bubbles can lead to economic instability and pose a significant risk to sustainable growth. In contrast, regions and industries experiencing slower economic growth face the opposite scenario. They often suffer from an outflow of resources that exacerbates their development dilemma and plunges them into a vicious cycle of decline.[88] This outflow not only affects the local economy but also has broader implications for global economic stability. Globalization has played a decisive role in the relocation of economic activities abroad through the liberalization of economic policies in numerous countries. The development of free and open markets and the free movement of capital and investment have significantly reinforced the trend toward

[87] Borio, C. E., & Lowe, P. W. (2002). Asset prices, financial and monetary stability: An investigation of the relationship. BIS Working Paper 114.

[88] Sheng, L. (2014). Economic structure, cost outsourcing, and global imbalances. The Journal of Australian Political Economy, 74, 81–94.

offshoring.[89] This process enables companies to optimize their operations by relocating certain functions to countries where they can save costs. However, it also raises complex questions about the economic security and long-term viability of national economies in the face of such global interdependence. The interplay between capital flows and offshoring illustrates the delicate balance that nations must strike in a rapidly changing global economy, a balance that is difficult to achieve.

Furthermore, globalization has greatly facilitated the spread of technology and knowledge across the world. This transformation process has expanded the diffusion of technology across borders in two main ways. First, globalization has simplified access to foreign knowledge, enabling countries to tap into a wealth of information, expertise, and innovative practices that were previously inaccessible. Second, it has intensified international competition, notably through the rise of companies from emerging economies. This competitive environment provides incentives for companies to innovate and adopt foreign technologies, ultimately promoting a culture of continuous improvement and adaptation. The sophisticated technology and management know-how of industrialized countries have spread rapidly to developing countries, boosting their productivity and competitiveness. Emerging economies are increasingly tapping into available foreign knowledge and technologies to enhance their innovation capacity and labor productivity growth. For example, for an average national sector, the flow of knowledge from technology leaders contributed around 0.7 percentage points of labor productivity growth per year during the 2004–2014 period, corresponding to about 40% of average productivity growth.[90] An important factor in building the innovation capacity of emerging economies is their increasing participation in global supply chains alongside multinational companies, although not all of them benefit as multinational companies.

Nevertheless, this inequality in technology diffusion means that some countries have been able to increase their industrial competitiveness relatively quickly, while others have made slower progress. The theory of

[89] Hobela, V. (2020). Economic offshoring in national economic security. Scientific Horizons, 23(12), 109–120.

[90] Aqib, A., Johannes, E., Giang, H., Florence, J., & Roberto, P. (2018, April 9).Globalization helps spread knowledge and technology across borders. IMF BLOG. https://www.imf.org/en/Blogs/Articles/2018/04/09/globalization-helps-spread-knowledge-and-technology-across-borders.

cyclical cumulative causation was first proposed by the economist Gunnar Myrdal to explain the phenomenon of uneven economic development between regions. According to this theory, differences in economic development will gradually increase in some regions due to different starting conditions and the "echo effect" (i.e., advantageous regions attract an influx of factors such as resources and talents, leading to a development gap in surrounding areas). However, when the level of economic development reaches a certain threshold, the "diffusion effect" (i.e., the spread of resources and factors from advantageous areas to surrounding areas) will gradually take hold, which will help to reduce the differences in economic development between regions.

In reality, the "echo effect" often precedes, or even exceeds, the "diffusion effect," which also leads to a gap in technological and economic development between industrialized and developing countries. As Feenstra and Hanson (1997) argue, the uneven diffusion of technology allows different nations to occupy different positions and degrees of participation in the industrial chain. Some countries focus primarily on low value-added processing, often limited to manufacturing and assembly tasks, while other countries dominate higher value-added segments, including R&D, design, and branding. This unequal participation promotes global economic imbalances, with wealth and technological progress concentrated in a few nations while others are left behind.[91]

Furthermore, since the third technological revolution since 1950s, some studies have argued that technology and innovation are difficult to transfer across geographical areas, which further exacerbates inequalities. According to dynamic agglomeration economies, geographic proximity facilitates the continuous and rapid exchange of new ideas on technical, organizational, and other improvements.[92] This means that once production is relocated, knowledge and innovation do not simply migrate across borders and automatically follow. Although the effects of globalization go beyond trade and finance and have led to massive changes in production,

[91] Feenstra, R. C., & Hanson, G. H. (1997). Foreign direct investment and relative wages: Evidence from Mexico's maquiladoras. Journal of International Economics, 42(3-4), 371-393. https://doi.org/10.1016/S0022-1996(96)01475-4.

[92] De La Ronde, C., & Swann Jr, W. B. (1998). Partner verification: Restoring damaged images of our intimate partners. Journal of Personality and Social Psychology, 75(2), 374. https://doi.org/10.1037/0022-3514.75.2.374.

this cannot help close the large international gaps in knowledge and innovation. For industrialized countries, the spatial attachment of innovation may encourage attempts to maintain their technological superiority; for developing countries, however, the spatial attachment of innovation can fundamentally limit their sources of growth and thus perpetuate global inequalities.[93]

The consequences of these imbalances are far-reaching. Countries that remain stuck in low value-added activities often face stagnant wages and limited opportunities for economic growth. This can lead to an increase in poverty and social unrest as citizens of these countries struggle to achieve a better standard of living. In contrast, nations that master advanced technologies and high-value sectors often benefit from increased productivity and innovation, further widening the gap. Dependency theory argues that developing countries are in a dependent position in the global economic system and that their economic development is controlled and influenced by industrialized countries. In the process of globalization, developing countries are often unable to fully control their own economic development; they can only passively accept the rules and standards of industrialized countries. This dependence not only limits the economic growth potential of developing countries but also exacerbates global economic imbalances.

As these countries continue to invest in R&D, they create a cycle of growth from which less developed countries find it difficult to escape. Furthermore, inadequacies in trade rules and the global financial system exacerbate these inequalities. New institutional economics emphasizes the importance of institutions for economic development. In the wake of globalization, institutional inadequacies and inequalities have exacerbated imbalances in the global economy. Industrialized countries occupy a dominant position in the global economic system thanks to their perfect institutional systems and strong institutional execution. In contrast, developing countries often face the problem of inadequate institutions and poor implementation. Such institutional differences not only limit the economic growth potential of developing countries but also exacerbate the North–South economic divide. Certain countries, especially those with significant economic influence, use their financial systems to adopt

93 Ernst, D. (2000). Carriers of cross-border knowledge dissemination: Information technology and global production networks. East-West Center Discussion Paper.

protectionist measures that shield their markets from foreign competition. These measures disrupt the natural order of trade and favor domestic industries while hindering the growth prospects of others. Such barriers limit developing countries' ability to access advanced technologies and markets, trapping them in a cycle of dependence and underdevelopment. The unequal distribution of technologies, combined with protectionist measures and flawed trading systems, creates a divide that undermines not only economic growth but also social stability and global cohesion. To address these imbalances, joint efforts are needed to create fairer trade practices and improve access to technology for all nations, so that the benefits of globalization are distributed more equitably across the world.

CHAPTER 2

Deindustrialization and Offshore Outsourcing in the United States

In today's globalized economic landscape, the history of US economic development is an important area of research. Changes in the economic structure of the United States, as a prominent participant and even dominant player in the global economy, have profound implications for the global economy. The closely intertwined phenomena of deindustrialization and offshoring have not only changed the industrial structure and employment structure of the United States itself but also triggered a series of chain reactions on a global scale. Deindustrialization, characterized by a decline in manufacturing jobs, has led to a shift toward service-oriented industries and created economic vulnerabilities. At the same time, offshoring has allowed companies to move production to countries with lower labor costs, further exacerbating domestic job losses. This dynamic has not only weakened the US manufacturing base but has also contributed to growing income inequality and economic disruption affecting workers and communities. Furthermore, the effects are being felt worldwide as developing countries become increasingly integrated into global supply chains, often at the expense of their own labor standards and economic stability. Understanding these intertwined phenomena is therefore essential to grasping the complexity of current global economic interactions.

Specifically, "deindustrialization" refers to a gradual decline in the share of manufacturing in the economy and a relative increase in the

E. Li Sheng, *A Recent History of Global Imbalances*,
https://doi.org/10.1007/978-981-95-1834-0_2

share of services. This shift is not accidental, but the result of a combination of factors. Four main causes of deindustrialization have been identified: (1) non-homothetic tastes, (2) technology, (3) outsourcing, and (4) international trade.[1] Technological progress has significantly changed production processes, making them more automated and intelligent, which has reduced the need for labor. Machines and software now perform tasks that previously required human intervention, leading to greater efficiency but also job losses in traditional manufacturing sectors. Meanwhile, increasing global economic integration has led to a gradual dismantling of trade barriers between countries, and companies have relocated their production to other countries and regions in search of lower production costs and larger markets.[2] As a result, developed economies like the United States are undergoing a transition toward deindustrialization that is affecting not only employment patterns but also the entire economic landscape. This transition has significant implications for workers, communities, and economic policy, raising questions about the sustainability of traditional manufacturing jobs and the future of work in a globalized world. Understanding these dynamics is critical for policymakers seeking to navigate the challenges and opportunities of this ongoing change.

Offshoring is a specific form of deindustrialization. Companies relocate part of their operations or production abroad to benefit from cheap labor, resources, and preferential policies in other countries or regions.[3] This model has reduced companies' operating costs to some extent, but it has also had an impact on the domestic labor market in the United States. While offshoring reduces production costs, it can also undermine domestic innovation capacity by shifting knowledge-intensive processes abroad. Research shows that when R&D activities are relocated, the "learning by doing" effect in home countries diminishes, which

[1] Van Neuss, L. (2018). Globalization and deindustrialization in advanced countries. *Structural Change and Economic Dynamics*, 45, 49–63. https://doi.org/10.1016/j.strueco.2018.02.002

[2] Rodrik, D. (2008). Industrial policy: Don't ask why, ask how. *Middle East Development Journal*, 1(1), 1–29. https://doi.org/10.1142/S1793812009000024

[3] Blinder, A. (2006). Offshoring: The next industrial revolution? *Foreign Affairs*, 85(2), 113–128.

can weaken long-term technological competitiveness.[4] When companies downsize their domestic workforce, especially in favor of cheaper foreign labor, wage levels stagnate or decline, disproportionately affecting low-skilled workers. While shareholders benefit from increased profits, the economy in general faces challenges as many laid-off workers struggle to move into higher-skilled positions that are not readily available. This discrepancy creates a cycle of economic uncertainty, as those who have lost their jobs due to offshoring often find it difficult to access new positions that require different skills or experience. Empirical studies confirm that offshoring reduces the wages of medium-skilled workers in the affected sectors by 4%–7%, while the impact on highly skilled occupations is minimal.[5] This exacerbates income inequality, as low-skilled workers face persistent wage pressure.[6] The result is a growing gap between the benefits enjoyed by a small number of corporate shareholders and the problems faced by a large proportion of workers. Understanding these intertwined phenomena is therefore crucial to grasping the complexity of current global economic interactions. Empirical studies confirm that trade liberalization under agreements such as the Regional Comprehensive Economic Partnership (RCEP) further accelerates offshoring by lowering trade barriers and transaction costs.

The study of deindustrialization and offshore outsourcing in the United States is of great importance for understanding broader trends in global economic development and the dynamics of industrial transfer. This study is essential not only for analyzing the specific challenges and opportunities facing the US economy in an increasingly interconnected world but also for understanding the broader implications of these phenomena for labor markets, economic policy, and social structures. By examining the effects of deindustrialization and offshoring, we can better understand how regions can adapt to economic change, mitigate negative consequences for displaced workers, and promote innovation

[4] Pisano, G. P., & Shih, W. C. (2012). *Producing Prosperity: Why America Needs a Manufacturing Renaissance*. Harvard Business Press.

[5] Levy, D. L. (2005). Offshoring in the new global political economy. *Journal of Management Studies*, 42(3), 685–693. https://doi.org/10.1111/j.1467-6486.2005.00514.x

[6] Autor, D. H., Dorn, D., & Hanson, G. H. (2016). The China shock: Learning from labor market adjustment to large changes in trade. *Annual Review of Economics*, 8, 205–240. https://doi.org/10.1146/annurev-economics-080315-015041

in emerging industries. Furthermore, this analysis provides a valuable case study for other countries facing similar challenges during their own economic transition. Policy measures such as the US Trade Adjustment Assistance program have had limited success, with only 37% of displaced workers finding equivalent jobs.[7] Alternative models, such as the German short-time work system, suggest that proactive skills development reduces long-term unemployment. The lessons learned from the US experience can help policymakers develop strategies that promote sustainable growth while meeting the needs of their workforce. Understanding these complex relationships therefore not only serves US economic policy but also enriches the global discourse on industrial development and economic resilience.

2.1 The Deindustrialization of the United States

The term "deindustrialization" essentially refers to the decline in the share of manufacturing in total employment.[8] Since the 1950s, the United States has experienced a societal shift in business and industrial transformation, with the decline of manufacturing and the rise of the service sector becoming defining features. This shift marks a fundamental change in the American economic landscape, in which once-thriving factories and industrial centers have been replaced by service-oriented industries. The service sector has grown due to factors such as the massive expansion of the financial sector and new forms of industrial organization that are promoting the disintegration of manufacturing through the outsourcing of many processes and functions that were previously performed in-house and are now considered services.[9] As manufacturing jobs have declined and often been relocated to countries with lower labor costs, the economy has shifted toward sectors such as technology, finance, and healthcare. This shift has not only altered the economic structure but also reshaped the social fabric of the United States.[10] Today, deindustrialization affects almost every corner of the country, but the relocation of companies

[7] U.S. Government Accountability Office. (2020). *Trade Adjustment Assistance: Outcomes Improved, but Few Participants Received Wage Subsidies*. GAO-20-502.

[8] Dávalos López, E. (2018). *Deindustrialization in the United States*. Voices of Mexico.

[9] Dávalos López, E. (2018). *Deindustrialization in the United States*. Voices of Mexico.

[10] Bluestone, B., & Harrison, B. (1982). *The Deindustrialization of America: Plant Closings, Community Abandonment, and the Dismantling of Basic Industry*. Basic Books.

outside the country has become much more common and affects salaried employees. Communities that relied heavily on manufacturing suffered job losses, leading to economic disruption and social problems, including growing inequality and a decline in middle-class stability. In urban areas, the number of jobs in the service sector has increased, but often at the cost of lower wages and precarious employment conditions. In the 1980s, layoffs mainly affected manufacturing workers, but in the 1990s, many white-collar workers were also affected, with massive layoffs at the country's largest companies. In 1991, General Motors laid off 70,000 employees, while IBM laid off 63,000 and AT&T laid off 40,000 at the end of the decade. In the spring of 1996, a *New York Times* investigation into job cuts revealed that 43 million jobs had been lost in the United States since 1979. In almost a third of households, at least one family member had lost their job.[11]

As a theoretical concept, deindustrialization has been extensively studied in the United States. The publication of Bluestone and Harrison's *The Deindustrialization of America* in 1982 placed the deindustrialization thesis at the center of their analysis. This book is considered the founding work of the theory and is frequently cited. Faced with increasing global competition and declining profit margins, companies have turned to cutting costs or diversifying manufacturing rather than modernizing older factories or pursuing technological innovation. The $6 billion takeover of Marathon Oil by US Steel in 1982 is often cited as an example. The *Deindustrialization of America* was published at a time when the unemployment rate in the United States had reached 10.8% in 1982, its highest level since the Great Depression. "As memories of the glory days after World War II quickly faded, many wondered whether the United States had lost its economic way," Bluestone later recalled.[12] The *Deindustrialization of America* has sparked considerable debate among politicians and economists. In Congress, the book was cited as evidence of the urgent need for an industrial strategy.[13] Mainstream economists have

[11] Minchin, T. J. (2006). "Just like a death": The closure of the international paper company plant in Mobile, Alabama, and the deindustrialization of the south, 2000–2005. *Alabama Review*, 59(1).

[12] Cowie, J., & Heathcott, J. (Eds.). (2003). *Beyond the Ruins: The Meanings of Deindustrialization*. Cornell University Press.

[13] High, S. (2023). The radical origins of the deindustrialization thesis: From dependency to capital flight and the abandonment of community. *Arbeit: Journal of Canadian*

almost unanimously rejected Bluestone and Harrison's analysis. In 1984, Robert Samuelson equated deindustrialization with "disinformation" in *The Washington Post*, saying it was "one of those portmanteau words that has crept into the language and should be thrown out."[14] The harshest criticism came from Lawrence, who called deindustrialization a myth, citing aggregate production and employment data. Specifically, Lawrence argues that the real number of manufacturing jobs in the United States did not decline between 1973 and 1980.[15] American historians also began to address the deindustrialization thesis during these years.[16]

In the early stages of economic development, many countries experience a rise in manufacturing, while primary sectors such as agriculture and fishing decline. This transition, known as industrialization, is characterized by increased investment in capital and intermediate goods, which promotes the growth of the manufacturing sector and facilitates structural reforms. However, as these reforms progress and the economy continues to grow, the importance of the manufacturing sector declines, leading to a greater emphasis on the service sector.[17] Another reason for the growth of the service sector is the change in demand. From a consumer's point of view, Engel's law states that a person's relative income spent on food decreases as their income increases, while they spend more on services, such as entertainment, especially in developed countries (i.e., the income elasticity of demand for services is higher than that for goods, making the service sector more dynamic). Consequently, this development leads to a phase of deindustrialization within the growing economy.

Industrialization and deindustrialization are economic phenomena that occur at different times but are closely related. Industrialization played a central role in the modernization of early developed countries. The Global

Labour Studies/Le Travail: Revue d'Études Ouvrières Canadiennes, 91, 31–56. https://doi.org/10.52975/llt.2023v91.005

14 Samuelson, R. J. (1984, May 30). Deindustrialization is a misinformation. *Washington Post*.

15 Lawrence, R. Z. (1983). The myth of U.S. deindustrialization. *Challenge*, 26(5), 12–21. https://doi.org/10.1080/05775132.1983.11470876

16 Marcus, I. M. (1985). The deindustrialization of America: Homestead, a case study, 1959–1984. *Pennsylvania History: A Journal of Mid-Atlantic Studies*, 52(3), 162–182. https://www.jstor.org/stable/27773053

17 Kang, S. J., & Lee, H. (2011). Foreign direct investment and deindustrialization. *The World Economy*, 34(2), 313–329. https://doi.org/10.1111/j.1467-9701.2010.01324.x

Industrial Revolution paved the way for industrialization in Western countries and widened the development gap between Western countries and the rest of the world. Between 1820 and 1950, the per capita GDP of Latin American countries fell from 60 to 40% of the Western value, that of African countries fell from 34 to 14%, and that of Asian countries fell the most, from half to 1/10.[18] In view of these significant differences, developing countries began to formulate their own industrialization strategies in the 1950s and embarked on the path of economic catch-up. These strategies often included measures to improve local production capacities, attract foreign investment, and improve education systems to attract skilled workers. Meanwhile, Western nations, especially the United States, entered a phase of deindustrialization.

This process involved the relocation of low value-added manufacturing sectors and traditional heavy industries, often associated with significant environmental damage, to regions with lower production costs. This shift was not only an economic decision but also a response to rising labor costs and regulatory pressure in Western countries. The shift of manufacturing jobs to developing countries has allowed Western economies to focus more on high-value services and technology-oriented industries, but it has also led to job losses and economic challenges at home. While developing countries have continued to industrialize to bridge the gap, the ongoing deindustrialization in the West reflects a complex interplay of economic strategies that have shaped global trade and labor markets. This dual process continues to influence global economic dynamics today and illustrates how the historical developments of industrialization and deindustrialization are intertwined in shaping the economic landscapes of nations.

Deindustrialization is an inevitable consequence of economic development that has reached an advanced stage. It is primarily driven by several interrelated factors, including high labor productivity, changing consumer demand, and the forces of economic globalization. Technological progress plays a central role in this transformation by significantly increasing labor productivity and leading to a decrease in the demand for human labor in the manufacturing sector. Machines and automation are gradually replacing traditional workers and fundamentally changing

[18] Nayyar, D. (2015). *Catch Up: Developing Countries in the World Economy*. Oxford University Press.

the workforce landscape. At the same time, the increase in living standards is leading to a remarkable change in consumer demand. People are beginning to prefer high-quality, innovative products over simple industrial goods, leading to a decrease in demand for traditional manufactured goods. In addition, consumers are increasingly attracted to high-quality products and services, reflecting the general trend toward a service-oriented economy. In this context, deindustrialization translates into a decrease in the share of the workforce employed in the manufacturing sector. Although the relative value added of manufacturing may persist in some advanced economies, its share of GDP is generally declining. This means that although fewer people are employed in manufacturing, the sector still contributes significantly to the overall value added of the economy.

Studies show that changes in consumer demand and increases in labor productivity are the main factors contributing to the decline in manufacturing employment in the United States. The literature shows that between 1970 and 2007, the share of manufacturing in employment in the EU15 fell from 28.2% to 15.6%, while in the United States it fell from 22.4% to 9.9%. Over the same period, the share of manufacturing in nominal value added in the EU15 fell from 26.6% to 18.1%, while in the United States it declined from 23.5% to 13.1%. These statistics highlight the declining role of traditional manufacturing in the economic landscape. Rather than a sign of decline, deindustrialization is indicative of a more knowledge-based manufacturing industry and a sign of the post-industrial era. As we transition into the post-industrial era, economies are increasingly focusing on advanced manufacturing techniques, R&D, and service-oriented sectors. This shift reflects an economic paradigm shift in which value no longer comes solely from physical goods but also from intellectual property and technological advances. Ultimately, this development reflects the adaptability of economies to global trends and the growing importance of a skilled workforce capable of thriving in a more complex and interconnected world.

With the continuous development of the US economy, tertiary industries such as the service sector and the financial industry have gradually become the main driving force of economic growth. The service sector has grown due to factors such as the massive expansion of the financial sector and new forms of industrial organization that promote the unbundling of manufacturing by outsourcing many processes and functions that were previously performed in-house and are now considered services.[19] These industries tend to have high value added and profit margins and attract large amounts of capital and labor, and the wave of economic globalization has promoted the optimal allocation of resources globally. Emerging economies, characterized by low labor costs and abundant resources, have attracted the relocation of numerous manufacturing industries.[20] This situation has put traditional manufacturing in the United States at a cost disadvantage, and many companies have moved their production overseas in search of higher profits. According to the US BEA, manufacturing value added in the United States declined from 16.1% of GDP in 1997 to 11.3% in 2018, while employment in the service sector accounted for more than 80.5% of total employment.[21] Over the past 60 years, an increasing share of employment and production has been provided by the service sector and a declining share by the goods sector. Figure 1A shows absolute employment figures by sector since 1950. Employment in both the goods-producing and manufacturing industries peaked in 1979. Since then, employment in the goods sector has fallen by 22% and in manufacturing (not shown) by 37%. In contrast, employment in the service sector has risen by 361% since 1950. Figure 1B shows the share of expenditure by sector. In 1950, services accounted for just under 40% of US GDP expenditure and goods accounted for 50%. In 2015, services accounted for just over 60% of GDP expenditure and goods accounted for 30%. Over the same period, the share of jobs in the service sector rose from 48% to almost 70%, while the share of jobs in goods production fell from 40% to around 15% of non-agricultural employment.

In economic terms, there are some differences between countries where the service sector dominates and those where the manufacturing sector dominates. Economic recovery takes longer in service economies than in goods-producing economies. Unlike storable goods, services generally do not have inventories, which amplifies the volatility of the business cycle. The rise of service production and deindustrialization in the United States over the past half-century has extended the period of

[19] Dávalos López, E. (2018). *Deindustrialization in the United States*. Voices of Mexico.

[20] Sassen, S. (2001). *The Global City: New York, London, Tokyo*. Princeton University Press.

[21] Amsden, A. (2001). *The Rise of "The Rest": Challenges for the West from Late-Industrial Countries*. Oxford: Oxford University Press.

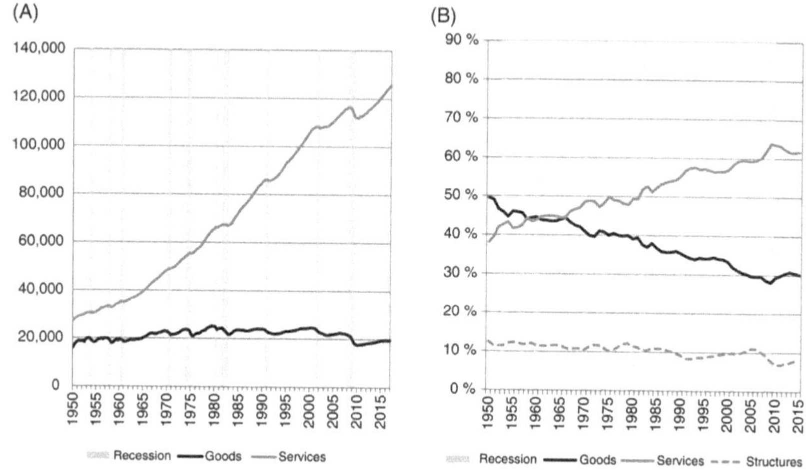

Fig. 2.1 The rise of services, deindustrialization, and the duration of economic recovery. *Source*: Olney, M. L., & Pacitti, A. (2017). The rise of services, deindustrialization, and the length of economic recovery. *Economic Inquiry*, 55(4), 1625–1647. https://doi.org/10.1111/ecin.12467

employment recovery from troughs to peaks in times of crisis by about 40%.[22] This is due to the rigidity of labor (services must be provided in person even during economic downturns), whereas in manufacturing, inventories can be reduced.[23]

In addition to the advantages of cost reduction, efficiency, and industrial modernization, deindustrialization poses challenges for the United States. Some analysts argue that deindustrialization merely reflects healthy economic development and indicates that economies evolve and adapt over time. In contrast, others suggest that it is a sign of major problems that need to be addressed urgently. Looking at the industrial structure, there has been a gradual decline in the share of manufacturing in the US economy. Many traditional manufacturing sectors in the United States,

[22] Olney, M. L., & Pacitti, A. (2017). The rise of services, deindustrialization, and the duration of economic recovery. *Economic Inquiry*, 55(4), 1625–1647. https://doi.org/10.1111/ecin.12467

[23] Felipe, J., Mehta, A., & Rhee, C. (2019). *Manufacturing Matters...But It's the Jobs That Count*. Cambridge University Press.

once a manufacturing powerhouse, are facing serious challenges. First, rising labor costs have put the US manufacturing industry at a competitive disadvantage, and many companies have decided to relocate their production to areas with lower labor costs to reduce production costs. Second, the rapid development of technology and innovation has led to dramatic changes in some traditional production methods and product demand. Some industries have been unable to keep pace with technological change and have gradually lost their competitiveness.

The shrinking industrial sector has led to the loss of a significant number of manufacturing jobs in the United States, which has had a profound impact on the national workforce. The general trend toward deindustrialization in the United States is evident in basic national labor market data. Total employment in manufacturing peaked at the height of World War II in late 1943, then fell back to pre-war levels as the country demobilized from the war, and continued to rise until the early 1970s. Thereafter, employment growth stagnated, finally peaking in 1979 and then beginning a slow decline that continued until 2000. At this point, the decline became more pronounced, with the country losing nearly 33% of its manufacturing jobs between 2000 and 2010. The "Rust Belt" states (e.g., Michigan, Ohio) suffered 45% more job losses than the national average, while manufacturing jobs were created in costal tech hubs.[24] Since then, there has been some growth in manufacturing jobs, although the shock of the COVID-19 pandemic in 2020 brought employment back to 2010 levels. The New Labor Forum highlights the alarming job loss figures and asserts that the fight for manufacturing is the fight for the heart and soul of the United States. This situation has profound implications not only for workers directly employed in the manufacturing sector but also for upstream and downstream industries. With manufacturing jobs declining, many workers are forced to face the harsh reality of unemployment or the challenges of reemployment. The new employment opportunities that are emerging are increasingly concentrated in sectors such as retail, hospitality, and other service-oriented areas. This shift has placed new demands on the skills and qualifications of the workforce, which must be adaptable and equipped with a diverse set of skills. Consequently, this development has placed increased pressure on social safety nets in the United States as more people seek help during their transition.

[24] Austin, B. (2022). *The Geography of America's Manufacturing Renaissance*. Brookings Institution.

"Deindustrialization has made it impossible for America to economically support a stable urbanized working class, leading to social and physical decay in cities that has been only partially mitigated by more recent urban gentrification and the accompanying service sector jobs."[25]

Deindustrialization has also led to regional imbalances in the United States. The development of deindustrialization in the United States is very uneven, varying considerably between regions. As industry in the United States has a strong regional, often city-based, economic organization model, deindustrialization is also a regional process. As a result, the consequences of deindustrialization in the United States not only affect individual workers but also exacerbate existing inequalities between different geographic areas, underscoring the need for targeted policy measures that address the specific challenges of each region.

Regional deindustrialization, which can be observed in various regions of a country, is another dimension of deindustrialization trends in both industrialized and developing countries. Regional deindustrialization is one of the major drivers of regional inequality in highly developed economies.[26] Economic activity and income are not distributed evenly across space. Marshall and Jacobs (1969)[27] emphasize intra- and inter-industry externalities, while Krugman (1991)[28] emphasizes the importance of unique historical characteristics of regions. Krugman's theory of new economic geography examines the regional distribution of manufacturing companies based on the economic growth of the manufacturing sector. This theory emphasizes that regions, rather than countries, are the true units of economic analysis. It states that most economic activities tend to concentrate geographically in a particular region. These theoretical approaches are important for understanding the nature of deindustrialization trends. The decline of manufacturing in a particular region inevitably leads to a deterioration of existing supplier, distribution,

[25] The Consilience Project. (2021, February 22). *Deindustrialization and the American City*. Feature Article. https://consilienceproject.org/deindustrialization-and-the-american-city/

[26] Meçik, O., & Aytun, U. (2018). Türkiye ekonomisinde erken sanayisizleşmeye bölgesel bir yaklaşım. A regional approach to early deindustrialisation in the Turkish economy. https://open.metu.edu.tr/handle/11511/58152

[27] Jacobs, J. (1969). *The Economy of Cities*. Random House.

[28] Krugman, P. (1991). Rising returns and economic geography. *Journal of Political Economy*, 99(3), 483–499. https://doi.org/10.1086/261763

and information links, forcing all surviving companies in the production chain to seek new information and customers. The success rate of this process determines the survival of the remaining companies and the development prospects of the entire region. At the same time, the reduction in supply in the labor market can lead to an increase in unemployment and trigger migration trends. As a result, deindustrialization accelerates in the regions.[29]

In light of the theory of new economic geography, industrialization in the United States historically began in the northern states (e.g., New England) and spread to other northern states from the early 1800s onward. The region's abundant mineral and water resources, its extensive railway network compared with other regions, and its large number of ports for foreign trade were the main factors driving industrialization in the region.[30] In contrast, productivity was very low in the southern states, where the agricultural sector dominated. California and Texas were able to attract industrial investment thanks to a combination of climatic conditions and energy resources with cheap labor.[31] The concentration of the automotive industry and Fordist-style production in the northeastern regions led to a large industrialization gap between the North and the South.[32]

Two factors characterize the process of regional deindustrialization in the United States. First, although the US economy is well integrated, there is heterogeneity across states in terms of labor composition and productivity. Second, the long-term performance of different regions in the United States varies. For example, New York, Boston, and the Sun Belt have experienced phenomenal economic growth over the past decade, while industrial cities in the Rust Belt have declined over the same period. These (negative) developments are linked to the local industrial structures of these regions: San Francisco and New York have developed

[29] Aralica, Z., & Stojcic, N. (2015). Regional patterns of deindustrialization and prospects for reindustrialization in South and Central Eastern European countries. wiiw Balkan Observatory working paper no. 118.

[30] Stone, L. B. (2017). *War and the Market Economy*. Vij Books India Pvt Ltd.

[31] Rodwin, L., & Sazanami, H. (Eds.). (2017). *Deindustrialization and Regional Economic Change: The Experience of the United States*. Routledge.

[32] Kollmeyer, C. (2018). Decline of unions, deindustrialization, and rising income inequality in the United States, 1947 to 2015. *Research in Social Stratification and Mobility*, 57, 1–10. https://doi.org/10.1016/j.rssm.2018.07.002

because they have increasingly specialized in emerging sectors such as IT and finance.[33] In contrast, Detroit has declined because it has traditionally specialized in heavy industries.[34] Figure 2.2 shows the regions where annual productivity growth exceeded 1% between 1978 and 2015. The figure shows that the northeastern regions are highly industrialized and productive, but the phenomenon of deindustrialization became apparent after 2004.

Some regions once dominated by manufacturing, such as the Rust Belt in the Midwest, have experienced significant economic difficulties in recent years. Since 2000, the share of manufacturing jobs has fallen from 25% to less than 10%. The Midwest was particularly hard hit, with manufacturing employment falling from 35 to 15% of the region's jobs.[35]

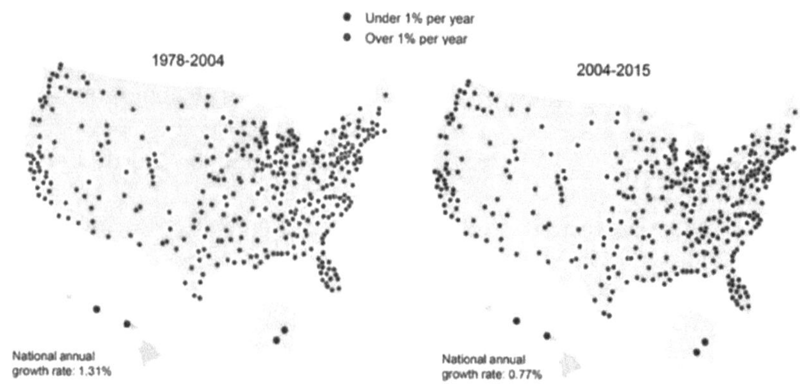

Fig. 2.2 Productivity trends in the United States. *Source:* Brookings' analysis of Moody's analytics data. https://www.brookings.edu/research/understanding-us-productivity-trends-from-the-bottom-up

[33] Yazgan, S., Marangoz, C., & Bulut, E. (2022). The turning point of regional deindustrialization in the US: Evidence from panel and time-series data. *Structural Change and Economic Dynamics*, 61, 294–304. https://doi.org/10.1016/j.strueco.2022.03.003

[34] Glaeser, E. L., Ponzetto, G. A., & Tobio, K. (2014). Cities, skills, and regional change. *Regional Studies*, 48(1), 7–43. https://doi.org/10.1080/00343404.2012.674637

[35] Green, G. P. (2020). Deindustrialization of rural America: Economic restructuring and the rural ghetto. *Local Development & Society*, 1(1), 15–25. https://doi.org/10.1080/26883597.2020.1801331

These areas are characterized by aging infrastructure, shrinking populations as residents move to other regions in search of better opportunities, and growing social problems that are becoming increasingly apparent. During the first half of the twentieth century, accelerated industrialization in the North prompted millions of African Americans to move from the rural South to northern cities—a massive demographic shift known as the Great Migration. They found employment opportunities en masse in emerging industrial professions, contributing to the growth of these urban centers. However, subsequent pressures of deindustrialization had devastating consequences, leading to ethnic unrest such as the infamous Detroit incidents of 1967. These events were symptomatic of deeper social tensions and economic instability. The consequences of deindustrialization have often led to a prolonged breakdown of public order, a situation that can be observed today in large parts of many post-industrial cities. As communities struggle with the loss of their industry, the decline in economic vitality has fueled a host of problems such as crime, poverty, and disinvestment, further complicating efforts to revitalize these once-thriving regions. This cycle of decline and instability underscores the urgent need for comprehensive strategies aimed at revitalizing both the economy and the social fabric of these affected areas.

In contrast, some regions of the United States, particularly those dominated by the financial, technology, and other service industries, such as the East and West coasts, have managed to maintain a relatively prosperous economic status. These areas benefit from a robust labor market and higher wages, largely due to the growth of tech companies, financial institutions, and service-oriented businesses that thrive in urban centers. However, this prosperity comes at a price. The country's deindustrialization has led to a significant increase in dependence on imported goods, as the decline in domestic manufacturing capacity has created an urgent need for large quantities of products from overseas. The semiconductor shortage of 2021 revealed that 78% of critical chips were imported, even though the United States produced 90% of the world's chips in 1960.[36] This dependence has led to a growing trade deficit, which not only reflects a trade imbalance but also exacerbates existing inequalities within the global economy. As the United States continues to import more than it exports, the effects are being felt across various sectors, highlighting the

[36] White House. (2022). *Building Resilient Supply Chains. 100 day Review under Executive Order 14017*

complexity of a post-industrial economy that increasingly relies on global supply chains. This shift raises important questions about sustainability, economic resilience, and the future of US manufacturing in a rapidly evolving global landscape.

Deindustrialization has different effects on urban and rural areas. Post-industrial theory suggests that there is a natural transition from agriculture to manufacturing and ultimately to the service sector. Rural areas, especially those that are small and not adjacent to a metropolitan area, do not have the population density and size to support many service sector jobs. Deindustrialization has led to the emergence of "rural ghettos"—areas where the poverty rate is above 20% and the employment rate below 60%.[37] These places face many of the same problems as urban ghettos, such as severe underemployment, selective migration, social isolation, drug use, and lack of services.

For several decades, attracting industrial companies has been an important strategy for rural development, particularly for creating businesses in low-skilled and low-wage industries. The availability and low cost of land and labor, and to a lesser extent tax breaks and other incentives offered by state and local governments, have attracted manufacturing companies to rural areas. Local authorities see rural industrialization as an important way to create jobs, increase incomes, and create new opportunities for the poor, especially those with low levels of education and skills. Job losses in manufacturing weaken the economic base of rural communities that depend on manufacturing and accelerate the selective migration of young, well-educated workers.[38] Households that remain face greater social isolation, which can lead to reduced social support, inadequate information about employment, and limited access to external resources. In addition, many rural areas experience more social problems, particularly drug use and crime. Deindustrialization stigmatizes rural slums and makes it difficult for businesses to establish themselves there, as employers may view workers' skills as obsolete. This stigmatization of rural areas increases the likelihood that businesses will not invest there and that young people will be less inclined to stay. Furthermore, the development of the service

[37] Green, G. P. (2020). Deindustrialization of rural America: Economic restructuring and the rural ghetto. *Local Development & Society*, 1(1), 15–25. https://doi.org/10.1080/26883597.2020.1801331

[38] Carr, P. J., & Kefalas, M. J. (2009). *Hollowing Out the Middle: The Exodus of Skilled Workers From Rural America and What It Means for the Nation*. Beacon Press.

sector in rural areas faces problems such as incomplete infrastructure and insufficient consumer demand; therefore, the service sector does not solve the problems caused by deindustrialization in rural areas.

In fact, there are differing views on the health of the US manufacturing sector and its impact on the economy. Some argue that US manufacturing is healthy and growing, pointing to indicators such as increased production and productivity. Others argue that the US manufacturing sector is in decline, pointing to the decline in manufacturing employment and the relocation of production and related functions to other countries.[39] Many of those who believe that US manufacturing is in decline argue that manufacturing capacity in the United States is being "hollowed out" as production facilities and support functions (e.g., R&D, IT, and accounting) are being moved overseas, leaving only the shell of a company in the United States. Some experts argue that the strength of a country's (or state's or region's) manufacturing sector depends on a "critical mass" of companies engaged in similar and complementary activities, and on positive and reinforcing factors (such as knowledge sharing, worker recruitment, start-ups, new factory locations, consolidation of supply chains, and infrastructure improvements) from this "critical mass" of companies. This creates a synergy effect that increases the overall strength of the cluster's companies. As US-based companies move their production and related activities to countries outside the United States, some argue that this "critical mass" could be lost, setting in motion a vicious cycle in which synergies are lost and companies choose to move their activities to countries outside the United States where such clusters have developed.

2.2 Obama's Policy Initiatives

Faced with the daunting challenge of deindustrialization, the Obama administration implemented a series of measures aimed at revitalizing manufacturing in the United States and reducing the trade deficit by actively promoting and facilitating exports. This strategic reorientation recognized the disproportionate contribution of the manufacturing sector to innovation, accounting for 70% of private-sector R&D spending

[39] Sargent Jr., J. F. (2012). The Obama administration's proposal to create a National Network For Manufacturing Innovation. https://hdl.handle.net/1813/78159

despite representing only 11% of GDP.[40] Despite these efforts, the effectiveness of these measures was limited by a variety of factors, including technological disruptions, fragmentation of the global value chain, and a persistent skills mismatch.

The US manufacturing industry has undergone a significant transformation, heavily influenced by outsourcing and offshoring in the context of globalization and economic liberalization. Recognizing the critical role that manufacturing plays in promoting economic growth and job creation, the Obama administration introduced the Framework for Revitalizing American Manufacturing. This comprehensive initiative aimed to restore manufacturing to a position of prominence in the US economy. The policy framework specifically targeted advanced manufacturing industries such as semiconductors and clean energy and established 16 Manufacturing Innovation Institutes (MIIs) through the National Network for Manufacturing Innovation (NNMI), in which the federal government invested $1 billion.[41]

To achieve this goal, Obama promoted a series of policy reforms.[42] The 2009 automotive industry financing program provided $80 billion in loans and equity investments and, according to an analysis by the Council of Economic Advisers, saved about 1.5 million jobs. At the end of 2011, Obama's Council on Jobs released a landmark report praising the important role of manufacturing in economic recovery and recommending stronger government support for the sector. In addition, in January 2012, the Department of Commerce published a detailed study highlighting the manufacturing industry as a cornerstone of the US economy and emphasizing its importance for job creation and innovation.[43] Following these developments, Obama's 2013 budget included a separate chapter outlining the need for subsidies for the automotive industry, as well as a proposal for various other incentives to promote manufacturing. These initiatives included tax breaks, trade adjustments, and support for R&D.

[40] Manyika, J., et al. (2012). *Manufacturing the Future: The Next Era of Global Growth and Innovation*. McKinsey Global Institute.

[41] White House. (2014). *President Obama's Plan for American Manufacturing*. Executive Office of the President.

[42] Obama, B. (2012). *State of the Union Address*. The White House.

[43] Bruce, B. (2012, February 17). Can Obama's manufacturing initiative really work? *The Fiscal Times*. https://www.thefiscaltimes.com/Columns/2012/02/17/Can-Obamas-Manufacturing-Initiative-Really-Work

These measures were intended to stimulate investment and promote innovation in manufacturing. As a result of these concerted efforts, the US automotive industry experienced an upswing, with some signs of recovery in the manufacturing industry as a whole. This renewed interest in manufacturing was aimed not only at creating jobs but also at improving the competitiveness of American products on the global stage. Overall, the Obama administration's policy initiatives were a significant step toward restoring manufacturing as an important part of the US economy.

The manufacturing industry plays a major role in the US economic system. Economically, manufacturing accounts for approximately 12% of US GDP and nearly two thirds of US exports. The manufacturing sector directly employs nearly 12 million American workers and indirectly supports millions more jobs in other industries (e.g., banking, shipping, insurance). It also finances about two thirds of industrial R&D in the United States, providing the foundation for the country's technological innovation and continued technological leadership. In addition, industrial workers earn higher annual salaries and benefits (averaging $77,186 in 2010) than non-industrial workers (averaging $56,436 per year). In the defense sector, the United States relies heavily on its manufacturing base to produce weapons, aircraft, vehicles, ships, and other equipment needed to protect the country.[44] Therefore, in his budget for fiscal year 2013, President Obama proposed the creation of the NNMI to accelerate innovation through investment in industry-relevant manufacturing technologies with broad application and to support the commercialization of manufacturing technologies by closing the gap between the lab and the market. The NNMI proposal called for the creation of up to 15 MIIs, funded by a one-time mandatory injection of $1 billion into the Department of Commerce's National Institute of Standards and Technology (NIST) and operated over a 10-year period. Each MII is composed of stakeholders from industry (including large corporations and small and medium-sized manufacturing companies), academia, federal agencies, and state agencies. The proposal called for each MII to be selected through a competitive process to serve as a regional center (and part of a national network) for manufacturing innovation focused on a specific area, such as advanced materials, manufacturing processes, enabling technologies, or industrial sectors.

[44] Sargent Jr., J. F. (2012). The Obama administration's proposal to establish a National Network for Manufacturing Innovation. https://hdl.handle.net/1813/78159

In terms of tax policy, President Obama actively encouraged companies to relocate their production to the United States by offering a range of tax incentives specifically aimed at manufacturing companies. This initiative aimed to increase domestic employment opportunities and stimulate economic growth by making it more financially attractive for companies to produce goods domestically rather than abroad. By reducing the tax burden on companies that chose to keep their production in the United States, the government sought to create a more favorable environment for job creation in the manufacturing sector. The American Recovery and Reinvestment Act, signed by Obama in 2009, was a cornerstone of this strategy. This comprehensive legislation provided incentives for private investment in various sectors by offering $2.3 billion in tax credits specifically earmarked for the manufacturing of clean energy technologies. These measures not only stimulated immediate investment in the manufacturing sector but also laid the groundwork for long-term growth and innovation in clean energy technologies. By promoting a sustainable manufacturing landscape, the Act contributed to a renewed focus on environmentally friendly production processes, which became increasingly important in the years that followed. These strategic measures were aimed not only at revitalizing the US manufacturing sector but also at positioning it for future success in an evolving economic landscape.

In addition, President Obama significantly increased investment in infrastructure development, recognizing that improved manufacturing and logistics conditions are critical to the success of the manufacturing sector. Modernizing key components such as roads, bridges, and transportation networks not only improves the efficiency of freight transportation in the country but also plays a critical role in reducing operating costs for manufacturers. By prioritizing infrastructure, the government sought to lay a solid foundation for future manufacturing growth and ensure that companies can operate effectively and competitively in an increasingly globalized market. This strategic focus on infrastructure also served to attract new businesses and promote innovation within the sector, contributing to a thriving economic environment. Furthermore, infrastructure investments create jobs not only in the construction sector but also in various related sectors, further boosting the overall economy and creating a cycle of growth that benefits communities across the country.

The Obama Administration also invested heavily in education and training, recognizing the importance of developing a highly skilled workforce capable of meeting the changing demands of modern manufacturing. This investment included a range of initiatives aimed at improving the skills and knowledge of the workforce. By putting in place appropriate training programs, apprenticeships, and vocational courses, the government ensured that people were equipped with the technical skills required in today's competitive environment.[45] The synergy between infrastructure modernization and workforce training was evident in advanced manufacturing centers, where modernized facilities were combined with adult education programs to align skills with Industry 4.0 requirements. In addition, scholarships and financial assistance were introduced to encourage young people to pursue careers in the manufacturing sector. These initiatives not only alleviated the financial burden associated with education but also gave students a sense of purpose and direction. By promoting science, technology, engineering, and mathematics (STEM) education programs, the government aimed to attract a new generation of skilled workers capable of driving innovation and technological progress in industry. In addition to formal education, partnerships with local businesses and manufacturing companies were promoted to provide students with hands-on experience and practical skills. This collaborative approach ensured that the education they received was relevant and directly aligned with employer requirements, thereby improving employability and productivity. Through these comprehensive efforts, the government sought to improve the technical level and innovation capacity of the entire manufacturing sector. These measures helped to increase manufacturing productivity in the United States by 2.1% annually between 2010 and 2016, despite persistent structural challenges such as geographic inequality.[46] This not only benefited the industry but also strengthened the economy, created jobs, and promoted long-term sustainable growth. Ultimately, by investing in education and training, the government laid the foundation for a dynamic and competitive manufacturing landscape capable of competing in the global marketplace.

In addition, Obama actively promoted a comprehensive overhaul of trade policy and sought to secure more favorable market access conditions

[45] Author, D. H., & Dorn, D. (2013). The growth of low-skilled service jobs and the polarization of the US labor market. *American Economic Review*, 103(5), 1553–1597.

[46] Crescenzi, R., & Rodríguez-Pose, A. (2012). Infrastructure and regional growth in the European Union. *Papers in Regional Science*, 91(3), 487–513.

and trade regulations for US manufacturing through extensive negotiations with other countries. His administration recognized the importance for the United States to remain competitive in the global marketplace. He therefore sought to renegotiate existing trade agreements to better serve American interests. Through dialogue with international partners, Obama aimed to establish trade practices that would benefit American manufacturers. In terms of energy policy, he strongly advocated for the development of clean energy and emerging energy industries, envisioning a future in which the manufacturing sector could rely on cleaner and more affordable energy sources. This strategic direction aimed not only to reduce the environmental impact of manufacturing processes but also to improve the overall competitiveness of the US manufacturing industry on a global scale. By promoting innovation in renewable energy technologies, his administration expected manufacturers to achieve significant cost savings, enabling them to operate more efficiently. To further protect American manufacturers, Obama introduced anti-dumping duties on Chinese products. This measure was intended to create a competitive environment favorable to the United States by reducing the competitive advantage of foreign goods sold at artificially low prices. In addition, the implementation of the "American-only Provisions" was intended to protect domestic industry from foreign competition, thereby strengthening the stability and growth of the US manufacturing sector. With these multi-layered strategies, the Obama administration sought to revitalize the US manufacturing sector and ensure its resilience in an increasingly competitive global economy.

The combined effect of these measures was clearly reflected in the growth of value added in the manufacturing sector in the United States. Between 2010 and 2019, this sector recorded an average annual growth rate of 1.8%, exceeding the level before the 2008 global financial crisis. This upturn indicates not only a recovery but also a revival of the manufacturing sector, highlighting the effectiveness of the targeted measures implemented during this period. In addition, manufacturing employment saw a remarkable increase from 11.595 million in 2010 to 12.934 million in 2022. This is an impressive V-shaped recovery that highlights the manufacturing sector's ability to rebound strongly in response to favorable conditions and investment. The increase in employment opportunities reflects a broader trend of economic revival, with skilled workers returning to jobs in a sector critical to the nation's economic fabric. In addition, the growth rate of private investment in manufacturing increased significantly, reaching an average annual growth rate of 4.4% over the 2010–2021 period. This shows a sharp increase in investor confidence, leading to a significant inflow of capital into the manufacturing sector. Such investments are essential for innovation, expansion, and modernization of facilities, which in turn boosts productivity and competitiveness. The trade dynamics further underscore this positive development. The growth rate of goods exports has accelerated considerably, averaging 5.3% per year between 2010 and 2022. This improvement suggests that US industrial products are gaining a stronger foothold in international markets, indicating improved competitiveness and the ability to effectively meet global demand. Taken together, these indicators paint a picture of a manufacturing sector that is not only recovering but also evolving to meet the challenges and opportunities of the present and position itself favorably in the global economy.

Obama's policy initiatives faced numerous challenges in their implementation, mainly due to the complexity of the global economic landscape. The international economic situation is complex and volatile, leading to limited success in trade negotiations. As various countries increasingly adopt trade protectionist measures, some barriers to US manufacturing exports have emerged. These protectionist measures not only restrict access of American goods to foreign markets but also have a domino effect that undermines overall economic growth.[47] Domestically, the political landscape is marked by deep divisions, with differing ideologies and interests hampering the implementation of such policies. The influence of various interest groups also hampers effective policy implementation and leads to inefficient resource allocation. After taking office, Trump reversed Obama's economic policies and pursued a protectionist trade policy that, while creating some new jobs, also strained the international financial environment and further exacerbated global imbalances. The Trump administration created a multi-layered policy framework to address the challenges of deindustrialization and offshore outsourcing. First, it imposed tariffs of up to 25% on $250 billion worth of overseas capital,[48] invoking section 301 of the Trade Act of 1974, and

[47] Gu, X.H., & Sheng, L. (2010) A sensible tool for Pareto-improvement: Capital Controls. Journal of World Trade, 44(3), 567–590.

[48] Sheng, L., & do Nascimento, D. F. (2021). *Love and Trade War: China and the US in Historical Context*. Palgrave MacMillan.

justified national security reasons for targeting China's "Made in China 2025" initiative, with semiconductor export restrictions on companies such as Huawei triggering a 12% drop in US semiconductor exports to China by 2019.[49] Finally, orders such as the "Buy American" guidelines raised domestic content requirements for federal procurement to 75%, temporarily reviving old industries such as steel. However, these measures had only limited structural effectiveness: while manufacturing production increased by 4.2% (2017–2019), job creation was concentrated in low-skilled sectors and the manufacturing trade deficit remained at $648 billion in 2019.[50] This synthesis highlights the tension between protectionist interventions and the realities of globalized production networks, revealing both short-term sectoral gains and systemic limits to reversing deindustrialization trends.

Furthermore, the effectiveness of government intervention and industrial policy has always been controversial from an economic perspective. Economic theory traditionally emphasizes the role of markets in guiding industrial development and structural adjustment. Furthermore, many scholars repeatedly point out that government intervention in markets is doomed to failure.[51] Many economists who share the general view that government intervention is an indispensable element of structural change reject industrial policy because there is no general framework that can serve as a guideline for policy-making.[52] Nevertheless, Obama intervened for two urgent reasons. First, it was urgent to find effective solutions to the dramatic economic and social problems caused by the ongoing international crisis. Second, there was a need to address some of the most important challenges associated with globalization: the process

[49] Semin, A. N., Kostyaev, A. I., Truba, A. S., Ponkratov, V. V., & Gagarina, M. V. (2019). Economic impact of the trade war between China and the United States on the Russian Federation. *China Economic Journal*, 12(3), 316–335. https://doi.org/10.1080/17538963.2019.1591573

[50] Findlay, R., & O'rourke, K. H. (2009). *Power and Plenty: Trade, War, and the World Economy in the Second Millennium*. Princeton University Press.

[51] Di Tommaso, M. R., Tassinari, M., Bonnini, S., & Marozzi, M. (2017). Industrial policy and the orientation of manufacturing in the United States: New methodological tools for strategic policy-making. *International Review of Applied Economics*, 31(5), 681–703.https://doi.org/10.1080/02692171.2017.1303036

[52] Lin, J. Y., & Monga, C. (2011). Growth identification and facilitation: The role of the state in the dynamics of structural change. World Bank policy research working paper no. 5313.

of internationalization of value chains and its impact on domestic industries, concerns about the relocation of production to the South, and fears associated with the rise of new industrial powers, to name only the most discussed issues.[53] Today, in both Europe and the United States, many politicians, observers, and academics advocate the need to define industrial policy strategies targeting specific industries (but also networks or technologies) to promote a wide range of economic and societal objectives.[54] In the words of President Obama, our times demand "strategic choices about strategic industries."[55]

Obama's policy initiatives provided subsequent US administrations with some experience and insights into managing deindustrialization and offshoring. They also enabled the public and governments to better understand the need to address this complex economic issue comprehensively, taking into account various factors. Following the Trump administration, the Biden administration, formed by the opposite political party, adopted remarkably similar perspectives and policies to deal with the effects of deindustrialization and offshoring. The Biden administration chose a multi-pronged strategy to combat deindustrialization and offshoring, combining industrial policy measures with job-related trade adjustments. At the heart of this approach was the CHIPS and Science Act (2022), which provides $52 billion for semiconductor reshoring and requires recipients to refrain from new investments in China for 10 years, a condition that reflects geopolitical and economic calculations.

At the same time, the Inflation Reduction Act (2022) ties $369 billion in clean energy subsidies to domestic content rules and mandates that 50% to 60% of electric vehicle and renewable energy components be manufactured in the United States.[56] These measures are in line with what Berger (2023) calls "productive protectionism," namely the use

[53] Di Tommaso, M. R., Tassinari, M., Bonnini, S., & Marozzi, M. (2017). Industrial policy and the orientation of manufacturing in the United States: New methodological tools for strategic policy making. *International Review of Applied Economics*, 31(5), 681–703. https://doi.org/10.1080/02692171.2017.1303036

[54] Bianchi, P., & Labory, S. (2011). Industrial policy after the crisis: Seizing the future. *Industrial Policy after the Crisis*. Edward Elgar Publishing. https://doi.org/10.4337/9780857930491

[55] Economist. (2010). The global revival of industrial policy: Picking winners, saving losers. *Economist*.

[56] U.S. Congress. (2023). Inflation Reduction Act: Labor provisions. CRS Report R47263.

of government power to rebuild the manufacturing ecosystem while imposing 25% tariffs on 818 Chinese imports. Labor requirements are enshrined in the "Good Jobs" regulation, which requires federal contractors to pay customary wages and provide training. Early results show that investment in the semiconductor industry increased by 120% year-on-year (Q2 2023), although critics note that 72% of new plants are located in already affluent districts,[57] meaning that regional inequalities persist. This strategy marks a break with the market-led approaches of the Obama era, instead embracing what Mazzucato (2021) calls the "entrepreneurial state" model, albeit with unresolved tensions between the logics of globalization and place-based reindustrialization.

2.3 The Growth of Offshore Outsourcing: Mainly in the United States

In the current global economic landscape, the rise of offshoring in the United States is particularly noteworthy. With the rapid development of science and technology and the intensification of market competition, many companies in the United States have strategically relocated part of their production to countries and regions with significantly lower labor costs. This trend has made the United States a leading player in outsourcing transactions and has significantly affected both the domestic economy and international business dynamics. Remarkably, the United States alone accounted for an astonishing 84.2% of the total $92.5 billion spent worldwide on business process outsourcing (BPO) services. This figure underscores the country's dominant role in shaping the outsourcing market. At the regional level, North and South American Continents together attracted about 42% of offshore outsourcing buyers. This statistic highlights the importance of North and South America in the global outsourcing ecosystem and reflects strong demand for low-cost labor and specialized services. Companies from various sectors, from IT to customer service, are increasingly turning to offshore partners to increase their efficiency, reduce their operating costs, and access a wider talent pool.

[57] Brookings Institution. (2023). *The Geography of the CHIPS Act*. Metropolitan Policy Program.

A 2005 study shows that US companies' activities abroad complement their domestic activities. The study focuses on the 1982–1999 period and finds that for every $10 invested by US manufacturing companies abroad, $15 flowed back to the United States. In addition, for every $10 in additional wages paid to foreign employees, $18 was invested in the wages of domestic employees.[58] Offshoring also makes companies more profitable. According to Deloitte's 2022 report, every dollar invested in offshoring yields a return of $1.28 for US companies. Furthermore, India makes a profit of $33 for every US dollar outsourced. Overall, the profit for every dollar invested is $12 net or $1.47 gross.[59] Daniel Drezner summarizes this effect in his article "The Outsourcing Bogeyman" as follows: "Thanks to outsourcing, US companies are saving money and becoming more profitable, which benefits shareholders and increases returns on investment."[60] This trend continues and presents both opportunities and challenges for the US economy, particularly in terms of job creation and the competitiveness of domestic industries.

Using case studies, researchers summarize the outsourcing process in the United States. Although the goals of outsourcing vary depending on the cases studied, the process is similar. Once management has made the decision to move a project overseas, the offshore supplier is selected and the project is initiated through a meeting between the offshore supplier's engineering team and the US customer at the customer's US office to discuss the division of the project scope, project schedule, and design criteria. In the design phase, there are three important milestones to monitor the progress of the project: the 30% review, the 60% review, and the 90% review. The supplier's engineers work in the US engineering office until the 30% review is complete, after which the supplier's offshore office completes the remainder of the design. Communication after the

58 Mankiw, N. G., & Swagel, P. (2006). The politics and economics of offshore outsourcing. *Journal of monetary Economics*, 53(5), 1027–1056. https://doi.org//10.1016/j.jmoneco.2005.07.016.

59 Marchant, M. A., & Kumar, S. (2005). An overview of foreign direct investment and outsourcing in the United States. *Review of Agricultural Economics*, *27*(3), 379–386. https://www.jstor.org/stable/3700863

60 Fennell, H. D. (2007). The significance of outsourcing and offshoring in the United States. University of Tennessee – Knoxville Dissertation.

30% review takes place via infrequent phone calls, daily email exchanges, and weekly design document production.[61]

This shift from the US office to the offshore office is primarily aimed at reducing costs and improving operational efficiency. By outsourcing functions that are not part of their core business, these companies can better focus their resources and efforts on improving their core areas of activity, thereby strengthening their competitive position in the market. Numerous tech companies, for example, have decided to outsource their production processes to focus on R&D and innovation. This approach not only accelerates the introduction of new products and services but also promotes a culture of continuous improvement and agility within the company.

In addition to outsourcing, companies are investing heavily in strengthening their supply chain management and optimization strategies. By establishing close cooperative relationships with outsourcing partners, companies can ensure a more stable and efficient supply chain that mitigate potential risks associated with offshoring, such as disruptions or quality control issues. Furthermore, the political environment in the United States has significantly contributed to the growing trend toward offshoring over the years. Various government measures may set higher operational thresholds for companies wishing to operate domestically, while providing incentives and support for offshore investment and production. Such a regulatory environment makes it increasingly attractive for companies to outsource their activities to other countries, thereby positioning themselves for greater success in a competitive global economy. This strategic shift not only increases profitability but also promotes innovation and makes US companies more adaptable and resilient to changing market demands.

The location strategies used for offshoring have become more diverse as transportation and communication technologies have matured, expanded, and spread to many parts of the world.[62] The competitive advantage of English-speaking countries like India (particularly with regard to call center activities for the United States) is now threatened on

[61] Nayak, N. V., & Taylor, J. E. (2009). Offshore outsourcing in global design networks. *Journal of Management in Engineering*, 25(4), 177184. https://doi.org/10.1061/(ASCE)0742-597X(2009)25:4(17

[62] Cobb, S. C. (2009). Redefining "offshore" in Latin America. *Growth and Change*, 40(2), 332–356. https://doi.org/10.1111/j.1468-2257.2009.00478.x

two fronts. The relative costs of low-wage or unskilled labor are increasing in traditional countries like India, while internal competition in the provision of these services and, more importantly, higher-value services such as those found in the IS/IT sector are being produced in direct competition with the onshore world.[63] As mentioned in *The Economist*, "The Indian trio of Wipro, Infosys, and Tata Consultancy Services (TCS) has built an IT outsourcing industry that has moved into the upper market segments, gone global, and is pursuing leading companies from rich countries such as Accenture and IBM."[64] Outsourcing firms increasingly tend to compete with the activities of the home country.

The rise of offshoring in the United States had already emerged as a significant phenomenon of globalization before Donald Trump took office. This trend has been particularly pronounced in the IT and BPO sectors, where companies have increasingly sought to leverage the cost advantages and expertise available in other countries. India, in particular, has become a popular offshore outsourcing destination, known for its large pool of skilled workers and strong English language skills. This linguistic advantage facilitates communication and collaboration, enabling US companies to maintain high service standards while reducing operating costs.

Besides India, China has become an important destination for US offshoring. The country has a large labor pool and robust manufacturing infrastructure, which has attracted numerous US companies looking to outsource various functions. Many US companies have chosen to transfer their manufacturing processes, assembly lines, production tasks, and procurement operations to Chinese manufacturers. This shift has enabled these companies not only to benefit from lower labor costs but also to take advantage of China's advanced manufacturing capabilities and supply chain networks. As a result, the offshoring trend has not only changed the landscape of US companies but has also had a profound impact on the global economy. Specifically, it facilitates the creation of complex global supply chains, increases productivity, and fosters innovation, as companies can focus on their core competencies and outsource routine tasks. Overall, this dynamic transformation of business processes underscores

[63] Range, J. (2008). Rethinking the Indian back office. *The Wall Street Journal*.

[64] The Economist. (2008, January 10). The challengers: Multinational companies from emerging economies. *The Economist*, pp. 12–13.

the interconnectedness of the global market and the strategic decisions companies must make to remain competitive. However, as outsourcing expands and deepens, it also poses development challenges for the US manufacturing sector and for scientific and technological innovation. Over the past 20 years, US manufacturing companies have radically shifted their R&D investment strategies toward an increasingly global orientation. Some countries have maintained the same R&D intensity as in 1960, while others have steadily increased their R&D spending as a share of GDP. Although domestic companies' R&D spending as a share of GDP increased during most of this period, this share has begun to decline. Today, their R&D spending outside the United States is growing at a rate almost three times higher than their domestic spending. In addition, US manufacturing companies have increasingly focused the composition of their R&D portfolios on short-term goals, meaning that the so-called "valley of death" (i.e., barriers to investing in radically new technologies that have the greatest long-term potential) is widening.[65] As a result, the US manufacturing sector is facing serious problems. The United States has had a manufacturing trade deficit for more than three decades, and the situation has worsened since 2000, rising from $240 billion to $1.2 trillion in 2022.

However, the interactive relationship between this type of trade cooperation and the development of national economies and societies is very complex. Although some economic theories support this trade activity, scholars still point out that the biggest beneficiaries of this trade activity are companies rather than countries, and that different types of job outsourcing will have different impacts on national economic development and employment. Furthermore, while many economists acknowledge that trade and other forms of globalization can cause painful disruptions for workers who must adapt to the changing employment structure of the country, they agree to benefit the country as a whole

[65] Tassey, G. (2010). Reasons and mechanisms for the revival of R&D strategies in the US manufacturing industry. *The Journal of Technology Transfer*, 35, 283–333. https://doi.org/10.1007/s10961-009-9150-2

because they enable companies to sell a wider variety of higher-value products at lower prices to US consumers and expand markets for US firms as developing countries increase their demand for US-made goods.[66,67]

However, it has been questioned whether this argument also applies to outsourcing services. For example, Milberg et al. (2007) argue that companies that outsource service activities may be the main beneficiaries, using profits from lower input costs to increase dividends to shareholders, raise share prices through buybacks, and engage in more mergers and acquisitions than reinvestments, thereby contributing to the growth of the US economy.[68] However, other scholars point out that the relocation of service jobs to other countries may have different implications for the labor market and public policy than the relocation of manufacturing jobs. Factory workers (e.g., textile machine operators) typically have less than 12 years of schooling or at most a high school diploma. According to the U.S. Bureau of Labor Statistics, administrative and professional workers are much more likely to have taken college courses or at least earned a bachelor's degree.[69] The exodus of service jobs will be accompanied by an educational migration that will reduce the number of jobs available, leaving American college students facing an employment dilemma.

The impact of globalization on the wages of American workers is often overlooked, even though it is significant. Some studies suggest that outsourcing increases wages in the United States. Offshoring also increases real wages for American jobs in general because it creates more jobs in high-skilled fields. The United States has a comparative advantage over other countries in terms of highly skilled workers, so jobs in the United States naturally pay better.[70] Outsourcing low-skilled, low-paid jobs, such as in manufacturing and call centers, allows more resources to

[66] Jackson, J. K. (2013). Foreign direct investment in the United States: An economic analysis. Congressional Research Service, 21857.

[67] Levine, L. (2012). Offshoring (or offshore outsourcing) and job losses among US workers. Congressional Research Service, 32292.

[68] Milberg, W., Mahoney, M., Schneider, M., & von Arnim, R. (2007). Dynamic gains from the offshoring of US services: A critical view. In Paus, E. *Global Capitalism Unbound: Winners and Losers from Offshore Outsourcing* (pp. 77–93). Palgrave Macmillan US. https://doi.org/10.1057/9780230608849_5

[69] Levine, L. (2012). Offshoring (or offshore outsourcing) and job losses among US workers. Congressional Research Service, 32292.

[70] Fennell, H. D. (2007). The significance of outsourcing and offshoring in the United States. University of Tennessee – Knoxville Dissertation.

be devoted to higher-skilled, higher-paid jobs. However, this has led to a shortage of low-paying jobs in the United States, causing many low-skilled and poorly educated people to lose their jobs, which in turn leads to high unemployment and income polarization. The outsourcing of jobs to low-wage countries, combined with the influx of imported goods, has been linked to lower wages for American workers.[71]

This trend not only affects wage levels but also leads to a fundamental redistribution of the workforce. Specifically, many workers have moved from well-paying manufacturing jobs, which once offered stable incomes and benefits, to lower-paying jobs in other sectors. Indeed, to access new positions, they have had to accept significant pay cuts, exacerbating the economic challenges they face. The structural shift from high-paying manufacturing jobs to low-paying service jobs has transformed the US labor market. For example, more than 58% of workers laid off due to offshoring between 2010 and 2020 suffered wage losses of more than 20%, and only 15% returned to their pre-layoff income levels within five years.[72] Another study shows that two thirds of the people laid off due to offshoring earned less when they were rehired, with nearly 25% earning at least 30% less.[73] As a result, the wage gap between low- and high-skilled workers is widening in the United States. In 2015 alone, foreign subsidiaries in the United States hired 14.3 million workers abroad; if these outsourced jobs had remained in the country, they would have been enough to employ the 5.9 million unemployed Americans, plus 4.3 million part-time workers who want to move to full-time employment.[74] This scenario illustrates not only the potential for job creation but also the economic benefits that could result from keeping these functions in the country. Public opinion on outsourcing is overwhelmingly negative. Seventy-one percent of Americans believe that outsourcing has a negative

[71] Ebenstein, A., Harrison, A., & McMillan, M. (2015). Why are American workers getting poorer? China, trade, and offshoring. NBER working paper no. 21027. http://www.nber.org/papers/w21027

[72] Author, D., Dorn, D., & Hanson, G. (2022). On the persistence of the China shock. *Brookings Papers on Economic Activity*, 1–78.

[73] Marchant, M. A., & Kumar, S. (2005). An overview of foreign direct investment and outsourcing in the US. *Review of Agricultural Economics*, 27(3), 379–386. https://www.jstor.org/stable/3700863

[74] *Outsourcing Statistics 2024: In the US and Worldwide.* TeamStage. https://teamstage.io/outsourcing-statistics/

impact on the economy and the job market, and 62% support government intervention to ban outsourcing altogether.[75] It is also easy for public figures to claim that it is patriotic to buy American goods and to emphasize the importance of government protection of American jobs from offshoring.[76] However, banning outsourcing would be harmful to the US economy in that it would prevent the United States from benefiting from trade, cost American consumers more, prevent companies from focusing on their core competencies, and allow inefficient producers to continue operating. This widespread dissatisfaction underscores the urgency for policymakers to reassess the impact of outsourcing and develop strategies to protect domestic jobs. As globalization continues to advance, prioritizing the well-being of American workers is essential to promoting sustainable economic growth and securing jobs in the United States. Resolving these issues is critical not only for workers but also for the well-being of the economy as a whole. Trade and technological change are affecting the types of skills that US companies seek. Domestically, it is essential to promote and finance new ideas to facilitate the adaptation of the labor market. Otherwise, the US economy will not be able to fully exploit the potential of this new globalization of services. These measures include wage insurance, the portability of social insurance, and, above all, tax credits for education and training that rely on partnerships between workers and employers, as well as with local trainers and governments.[77]

In recent years, geopolitical and economic security considerations have prompted the United States to pursue a policy of nearshore outsourcing, with Mexico becoming the main beneficiary of this strategic shift. This change has resulted in significant shifts in the flow of goods and capital. For example, the share of US imports from China has fallen to its lowest level since 2006, while shipments from Mexico to the United States have increased by 20% compared with two years ago. The Peterson Institute attributes 40% of US nearshoring activity to geopolitical risks, with 60%

75 *Outsourcing Statistics 2024: In the US and Worldwide*. TeamStage. https://teamstage.io/outsourcing-statistics/

76 Fennell, H. D. (2007). The significance of outsourcing and offshoring in the United States. University of Tennessee – Knoxville Dissertation.

77 Mann, C. L. (2005). Offshore outsourcing and the globalization of US services: Why now, how important, and what policy implications. *The United States and the World Economy: Foreign Trade Policy for the Next Decade*,. Peterson Institute for International Economics, Discussion Paper.

of investment diverted from Asia going to Mexico.[78] This shift is not a coincidence, but a direct response to evolving national policies aimed at improving economic resilience. US companies quickly adapted to this new political direction. Between 2020 and 2021, the number of bids received by Mexican suppliers from large US corporations increased by 514%. During the same period, offers to Latin American suppliers rose by 155% overall.

These figures clearly show that US companies are increasingly abandoning traditional offshoring practices in favor of nearshoring, particularly in the manufacturing sector. Cooperation between US and Latin American supply chains in the area of nearshore outsourcing continues to develop at a measured but steady pace. As a result, Latin American high-tech exports are expected to grow by 12% annually after 2020.[79] The Biden administration made this focus on nearshore outsourcing even clearer, pursuing a broader strategy of strengthening economic ties with Latin American countries. Although Mexico remains the most important hub for these outsourcing efforts, other regions in Latin America are gaining importance, indicating a shift toward a more diversified approach. In addition, there is a notable shift in US–Latin American cooperation in supply chains, moving from low-end manufacturing to high-end manufacturing and services.[80] This development not only strengthens the competitiveness of both regions but also promotes innovation and cooperation.

While the United States is the main promoter of this nearshore outsourcing strategy, Latin America is also actively pursuing its own role in this framework. Brazil's Plano Nacional de IoT aims to capture 5% of the global Internet of Things (IoT) market by 2025, supported by US tech partnerships. This symbiotic shift underscores a recalibration of global supply chains that balances efficiency and resilience, and signals a mutual commitment to economic growth, stability, and shared prosperity in a rapidly changing global landscape.

[78] Hufbauer, G. C., & Schott, J. J. (2023). *Reshoring, Friendshoring, and the Future of Global Supply Chains*. Peterson Institute for International Economics.

[79] Lederman, D., & Maloney, W. F. (2023). *Does What You Export Matter? The Case of Latin America*. World Bank Publications.

[80] Zhang J.Y.. The "nearshore outsourcing" cooperation of the Meila supply chain: Current situation, motivation, and prospects. (mei la gong ying lian 'jin an wai bao' he zuo: xian zhuang, dong yin he qian jing). *Pacific Journal*, 2, 56–67.

In addition, analysts speculate that offshore production could be relocated to the United States. This conclusion is based on an analysis of the effects of high oil prices in the fall of 2008, the global recession, and the recent rise in trade protectionism. In his article "Freight Pain: The Rise and Fall of Globalization" in the November/December 2008 issue of *Foreign Affairs*, Mark Levinson notes that rising transportation costs and declining reliability are making long-distance supply chains less attractive. Levinson believes that companies that supply American and European customers with goods manufactured in Asia (China) will rethink their business models and look for ways to reduce the distance between the factory and store shelves.[81]

However, researchers believe that such repatriation is difficult from the point of view of the industrial chain. "Such considerations are far too simplistic to serve as justification for the repatriation of a single industry. Any leap from speculation to implementation would have to be based on the operational business model, supply chain, and availability of intellectual and production-related capital of each industry eligible for repatriation."[82] China's electronics industry is a particularly striking example of the complexity of the challenge of repatriating a key capability. It is estimated that the Chinese electronics industry generated 35% of global electronics industry revenue in 2008, or just over a quarter of China's GDP in 2008. Chinese electronics companies have taken steps to ensure that the electronics industry does not return to their home country in the foreseeable future through their own advancements in the value chain, the localization of the entire supply chain, and national and economic policies.

[81] Levinson, M. (2008). Freight pain: The rise and fall of globalization. *Foreign Affairs*, 87, 133.

[82] Pecht, M., & Zuga, L. (2009). China as the hegemon of the global electronics industry: How it got that way and why it won't change. *IEEE Transactions on Components and Packaging Technologies*, 32(4), 935–939.

CHAPTER 3

Theoretical Explanation and Empirical Analysis of Offshore Outsourcing

As international trade continues to grow and IT continues to evolve at a rapid pace, many companies are increasingly moving their business processes to different countries or regions. Coupled with the maturation of groundbreaking technologies such as cloud computing and 5G communications, cross-border business transactions have grown exponentially. According to data from the McKinsey Global Institute, 78% of Fortune Global 500 companies adopted offshore outsourcing strategies for their business processes between 2020 and 2023, achieving an average reduction in operating costs of 23% and an improvement in market response speed of 41%.[1] This strategic shift reflects companies' simultaneous pursuit of three goals in the age of Globalization 4.0: efficiency, resilience, and innovation. The goal is to significantly reduce costs, increase operational efficiency, and open up new markets for growth. While this cross-border distribution of resources opens up many opportunities for companies, it also comes with a number of challenges and problems.

The rise of offshore outsourcing is not a coincidence, but rather the result of a complex interplay of various factors. The advancement of global economic integration has significantly promoted closer economic

[1] McKinsey Global Institute (2023). Rethinking global value chains in an age of disruption. Company Report.

E. Li Sheng, *A Recent History of Global Imbalances*,
https://doi.org/10.1007/978-981-95-1834-0_3

ties between nations while gradually dismantling trade barriers. The new generation of trade agreements, including the RCEP, has reduced average tariffs in the Asia–Pacific region from 7.3% to 1.2%, creating a trade-generating effect worth $2.8 trillion. The removal of these institutional barriers has reduced the cost of cross-border business coordination by 34%, directly leading to manufacturing outsourcing exceeding $4.6 trillion in 2022.[2] This has created a favorable environment for companies to expand their cross-border business activities. At the same time, remarkable IT advances have transformed remote communication and collaboration, making them more efficient and extremely convenient. Cloud-native platforms for distributed collaboration (e.g., AWS Outposts, Azure Stack) have significantly improved the efficiency of real-time cross-border team collaboration. The application of blockchain smart contracts further reduces cross-border payment settlement cycles from 7 days to 8 hours, significantly reducing default risks. Technological innovations are redefining the limits of traditional outsourcing models and reducing the risks associated with conducting business in remote locations, encouraging more companies to explore outsourcing options as a viable strategy for growth and competitiveness.

However, the trend toward offshore outsourcing can bring significant challenges, including the potential loss of domestic jobs, which can have a profound impact on the local labor market. This shift can lead to unemployment or underemployment in certain sectors and adversely affect the livelihoods of many workers. Furthermore, differences in laws, regulations, cultural backgrounds, and business practices across countries and regions can pose significant barriers to effective management and business operations. To navigate this complexity, companies often have to invest significant time and resources to adapt their strategies, training, and communication methods, further complicating their business processes.

For scientists and policymakers, an in-depth examination of the offshoring phenomenon is of great theoretical and practical importance. By systematically analyzing and researching this complex topic, researchers can gain valuable insights that provide a solid scientific basis for business decision-making processes. Such analyses not only improve understanding of economic dynamics but also provide governments with the knowledge they need to formulate sound and effective policy

[2] Baldwin, R., & Evenett, S. (2023). *Collateral Damage: Trade Wars in a Fragmenting Global Economy*. CEPR Press.

measures. These policy measures aim to promote sustainable economic development and ensure social stability, ultimately fostering a more resilient economy capable of adapting to the challenges of globalization and changing labor markets. The implications of the study of offshoring thus go well beyond a purely academic interest and have real-world implications for both businesses and society as a whole.

3.1 A Theoretical Model to Explain Offshoring

By definition, "offshoring" refers to the relocation of certain business processes or services of a company to countries or regions located beyond its own borders. Value chain theory emphasizes that companies should focus on their core activities and outsource non-core activities to companies with professional advantages. This allows companies to focus their resources on strengthening their core competitiveness and on optimizing and upgrading the value chain. This shift involves much more than a simple change of geographic location; it encompasses a series of comprehensive decisions regarding resource allocation, cost considerations, strategic planning, and other critical factors. Companies typically choose offshoring as a strategic business approach to achieve various goals, such as sourcing higher quality resources, reducing operating costs, improving efficiency, and expanding into new markets. The advantages of outsourcing from a strategic perspective can be summarized as follows[3]:

1. To maximize the efficiency of internal resources by focusing on investments and engaging in core competencies;
2. To develop core competencies by building barriers against the company's current or future competitors seeking to enter its areas of interest, thus protecting its competitive advantages;
3. To use external firms' investments, innovations, skills, and specializations, which could be kept in-house through continuous investments and innovations;

[3] Quinn, J. B. (1994). Strategic outsourcing. *Sloan Management Review*. Magazine Summer, July.

4. To reduce risks in rapidly changing markets with advanced technologies; an outsourcing strategy reduces technology upgrade risks and R&D costs by shortening production cycles and making response to customer needs more flexible and faster.

In a broader context, offshoring can be seen as a strategic decision by companies seeking to maximize their cost efficiency on a global scale to remain competitive in an increasingly interconnected world. Multinational companies are increasingly outsourcing R&D to third parties, regardless of their location, to take advantage of cost benefits and scarce talent and thus create and maintain competitive advantages.[4] Offshoring is a consequence of the international division of labor and globalization, which leads to the relocation of economic activities related to services to regions where investments yield the highest returns.[5] Consequently, offshoring affects not only individual companies but also global supply chains and labor markets. To better understand the motivations and behaviors behind companies' offshoring decisions, a comprehensive theoretical framework can be provided based on TCT and RBT. TCT examines the costs associated with economic exchanges and helps companies decide whether to produce internally or outsource processes. In contrast, RBT emphasizes the importance of a company's internal resources and capabilities in achieving competitive advantage. By integrating these two perspectives, we can gain a better understanding of the complex dynamics that drive offshoring decisions, enabling more informed policy decisions and corporate strategies in the global market.[6]

TCT, also called transaction cost economics (TCE), is an important theoretical framework used to explain the nature, scope, and limits of companies within economic organizations. Originally developed by Ronald Coase, this theory was further developed by Oliver Williamson

[4] Parida, V., Wincent, J., & Oghazi, P. (2016). Transaction cost theory and coordinated protective investment in R&D offshoring. *Journal of Business Research*, 69(5), 1823–1828. https://doi.org/10.1016/j.jbusres.2015.10.063

[5] Jahns, C., Hartmann, E., & Bals, L. (2006). Offshoring: Dimensions and spread of a new business concept. *Journal of Purchasing and Supply Management*, 12(4), 218–231. https://doi.org/10.1016/j.pursup.2006.10.001

[6] Dunning, J. H. (1988). The eclectic paradigm of international business: A restatement and some possible extensions. *Journal of International Business Studies*, 19(1), 1–37.

and other influential scholars who enriched its fundamental content.[7] The research model includes three exogenous variables (i.e., contractor reputation, asset specificity, and uncertainty) and two endogenous variables (i.e., post-contract opportunism and outsourcing success).[8]

When describing transactions, TCT therefore relies on three key dimensions: the conditions required for the transaction in terms of asset specificity, the degree, and nature of uncertainty surrounding the transaction, and the frequency of transactions, although this is not generally recognized as a core dimension in all formulations of TCT. For example, some scholars emphasize asset specificity, uncertainty, and transaction frequency as decisive factors, while others focus on different combinations or additional elements. Although all three dimensions are important, asset specificity is particularly crucial for drawing refutable implications because it can strongly influence the choice of governance structures.[9] The theory is based on two behavioral assumptions: bounded rationality and opportunism. According to Simons's (1961) concept of bounded rationality, economic actors are "intentionally rational, but only rationally limited."[10] When rationality is limited, economic actors face uncertainties from various sources in their transactions, and complex contracts are therefore inevitably incomplete to some extent, which encourages the study of institutions.[11] "Opportunism" refers to the tendency of economic actors to pursue their own interests, which allows for deception. Combined with limited rationality, opportunism complicates organizational problems by increasing sources of uncertainty. Based on these two behavioral assumptions, the problem of economic organizations is to "organize transactions in such a way that limited rationality is exploited while protecting them

[7] Coase, R. H. (1937). The nature of the business. *Economic*, 4(16), 386–405.

[8] Wang, E. T. (2002). Transaction attributes and software outsourcing success: An empirical test of transaction cost theory. *Information Systems Journal*, 12(2), 153–181. https://doi.org/10.1046/j.1365-2575.2002.00120.x

[9] Riordan, M. H., & Williamson, O. E. (1985). Asset specificity and economic organization. *International Journal of Industrial Organization*, 3(4), 365–378. https://doi.org/10.1016/0167-7187(85)90030-X

[10] Simon, H. A. (2013). *Verwaltungshandeln*. Simon and Schuster.

[11] Williamson, O. E. (1989). Transaktionskostenökonomie. In Elsevier *Handbook of Industrial Organization* (pp. 135–182). https://doi.org/10.1016/S1573-448X(89)01006-X

from the dangers of opportunism."[12] Using the transaction as the unit of analysis, TCT thus considers companies, markets, and mixed forms as alternative forms of organization and views the division of economic activity among them as a decision variable.

TCE offers a comprehensive perspective for understanding the reasons for the existence of companies, the mechanisms through which they organize their internal structures, and the motivations that lead them to engage in various forms of economic transactions. One of the key areas where transaction costs play an important role is supply chain management, as they influence operational efficiency and strategic decision-making. TCT provides a theoretical basis for the strategic behavior of companies in international procurement decisions.[13] For example, Boehm (2015) argues that improving contract institutions reduces market transaction costs.[14] Companies driven by transaction cost rewards change their organizational boundaries and outsource internal activities to external suppliers.[15] This dynamic is referred to as outsourcing in the pursuit of greater efficiency and cost savings. The implications of TCT go beyond mere operational adjustments; they reveal how companies strategically manage their environment to optimize their performance. By focusing on transaction costs, companies can improve their adaptability in a rapidly changing market landscape, ultimately promoting their long-term success and competitiveness in the global economy.

In the context of offshore outsourcing, TCT primarily examines the economic principles underlying the decision to relocate business activities to foreign locations with a view to minimizing transaction costs. TCT assumes that the choice between internal production, outsourcing, or offshore outsourcing is about reducing transaction costs, including

[12] Williamson, O. E. (1984). The economics of governance: Framework and implications. *Journal of Institutional and Theoretical Economics*, H.1, 195–223. https://www.jstor.org/stable/40750687

[13] Berghuis, E., & den Butter, F. A. (2017). The transaction cost perspective on international supply chain management; Insights from case studies in the manufacturing industry in the Netherlands. *International Review of Applied Economics*, 31(6), 754–773. https://doi.org/10.1080/02692171.2017.1324409

[14] Boehm, J. (2015). The effects of contract enforcement costs on outsourcing and overall productivity. Working paper.

[15] Liang, Y. (2022). Effects of financial development on outsourcing and total factor productivity. *Journal of Development Economics*, 154, 102770. https://doi.org/10.1016/j.jdeveco.2021.102770

the costs associated with finding partners, negotiating contracts, monitoring performance, and enforcing agreements. In the case of offshore outsourcing, TCT suggests that companies can reduce transaction costs by taking advantage of certain locations characterized by low labor costs, professional skills, and regulatory incentives. By relocating some functional departments abroad, companies can typically reduce the costs of finding professional workers and benefit from more potential partners. Due to the fierce competition among service providers in offshore destinations, negotiation costs also tend to be low. In the market, companies have to spend a lot of time and resources searching for suitable trading partners and conducting complex negotiations to reach cooperation agreements. As professional third-party providers, outsourcing service providers usually have extensive industry experience and resource reserves that can provide companies with more convenient and efficient transaction options. Studies show that outsourcing can reduce search costs by up to 40% and negotiation costs by 30% compared with internal solutions.

Through outsourcing, companies can significantly reduce their search and negotiation costs to enter the market faster and seize business opportunities. In addition, the German Agency for Technical Cooperation argues that offshore outsourcing can promote greater transaction security through the standardization of contractual agreements and the use of the mature management framework of offshore locations. Blockchain technology, for example, enables standardized contractual agreements and transparent transaction tracking, which increases trust and reduces monitoring costs in cross-border outsourcing. This, in turn, reduces the monitoring and enforcement costs associated with cross-border transactions. Internal company transactions often involve high monitoring and enforcement costs, especially when multiple departments or teams are involved. The complexity of communication, coordination, and resource allocation further increases the cost burden. As outsourcing service providers represent an independent third party, their service quality, and efficiency are typically constrained by both market mechanisms and contractual terms. This helps reduce internal monitoring and enforcement costs and improve overall operational efficiency. The changing market environment and technological developments present companies with many uncertainties and risks. According to a 2025 survey, 82% of companies cited market volatility and technological disruption as key risks, with outsourcing being a primary strategy to mitigate these risks.

Outsourcing allows companies to transfer some of their non-core and high-risk activities to external service providers to spread risks and improve their risk management capabilities. At the same time, the expertise and experience of outsourcing service providers help companies to better respond to market changes and technological challenges. The example of Amazon and JD.com clearly illustrates the need and strategic value of outsourcing, based on the different decisions made by the two companies for their logistics business. Amazon decided to outsource its logistics business to professional third-party providers to reduce the costs of developing its own logistics system and improve efficiency. JD.com chose to build its own logistics system, which has particular advantages in the Chinese market environment characterized by relatively low labor costs and a mix of good and bad logistics companies on the market, making it difficult to guarantee service quality. However, in view of changes in the market environment and technological developments, JD.com is also consistently reviewing cooperation models with external logistics service providers to further optimize logistics costs and efficiency.

However, TCT also acknowledges that offshoring has brought new costs, such as cultural and communication barriers, currency risks, and potential compliance issues. Companies must therefore weigh these additional costs against the expected savings from reducing labor costs and other operating expenses. One example is Tesla's offshore outsourcing factories. Tesla plans to spend $2 billion to build a factory in India to reduce production costs and increase market share. However, this offshoring strategy faces numerous challenges in practice, leading to higher costs. First, the business environment in India is relatively complex and varies greatly in terms of laws, politics, culture, and other aspects, requiring Tesla to spend a lot of time and energy on adaptation and coordination. This not only increases the complexity of the project but also leads to additional costs. Second, India's infrastructure is relatively weak, particularly in areas such as energy, transportation, and logistics, which could negatively impact Tesla's production and operations. To ensure stable and efficient production, Tesla may need to invest more in infrastructure improvements, which will undoubtedly increase the cost burden. In addition, the Indian labor market has some challenges, such as insufficient skill levels and high labor mobility, which could negatively impact Tesla's production quality and efficiency.

To improve the skill level of its employees and maintain a stable workforce, Tesla may need to spend more on training and human resource management, which will also lead to higher costs. In short, TCT provides a cost–benefit analysis framework for corporate decision-making regarding offshore outsourcing. By leveraging the advantages of a particular location and reducing additional costs to minimize transaction costs, companies can optimize their operational efficiency and achieve a more cost-effective global presence.

According to statistics, cost savings are the main reason why companies resort to outsourcing, with 59% citing cost reduction as their motivation.[16] Large companies are the main proponents of offshore outsourcing, primarily to reduce labor costs. Due to increased price competition in Western markets, management has no choice but to look for the most effective cost control measures, making offshore outsourcing an inevitable choice. A growing number of companies have relocated some, if not all, of their production abroad, with design, R&D, and marketing being the only activities remaining in their home countries. Examples include Dell Computer, Gap, and many Italian clothing companies. In fact, some manufacturers now produce nothing in their home countries, which serve only to manage their global value chain.[17] This illustrates the crucial role that financial efficiency plays in corporate decision-making.

In addition to cost savings, there are other compelling reasons for outsourcing that enable companies to focus on their core business. By outsourcing functions that are not part of their core business, companies can devote more resources and attention to their main objectives, thereby promoting innovation and growth. In addition, 47% of companies are using outsourcing as a solution to capacity issues, as it allows them to cope with fluctuating demands without having to increase their internal staff. This flexibility can be crucial for maintaining operational efficiency during peak periods. Improving service quality is another reason: 31% of companies outsource to benefit from specialized expertise that improves customer satisfaction and overall performance. Finally, 28% of companies believe that outsourcing helps them meet specific business needs more effectively by giving them access to technologies or skills that may not

[16] Deloitte. (2022). 2022 Global Outsourcing Survey. https://www2.deloitte.com/content/dam/Deloitte/us/Documents/process-and-operations/us-global-outsourcing-survey-2022.pdf

[17] Pellicelli, M. (2018). Gaining flexibility and innovation through offshore outsourcing. *Sustainability*, 10(5), 1672. https://doi.org/10.3390/su10051672

be available in-house. Overall, these factors highlight the versatility of outsourcing as a strategic tool for modern companies seeking to optimize their operations and gain a competitive advantage in the marketplace.

RBT originated in the field of strategic management in the 1980s. Its original intention was to explain why some companies are able to achieve sustained competitive advantages in a highly competitive market environment. During its early development, the theory received significant contributions from strategic management scholars such as Wernerfelt and Barney. Wernerfelt (1984) first introduced the resource-based view (RBV) into his classic resource-based theory of the firm. These resources are valuable, scarce, inimitable, and irreplaceable, and can therefore be a source of competitive advantage for companies.[18]

Barney (1991) further develops RBT and proposes the value, rarity, imitability, and organization (VRIO) framework to assess whether corporate resources can provide companies with sustainable competitive advantages. He argues that resources can only become the basis of sustainable competitive advantages for companies if they simultaneously possess the following four attributes: value, scarcity, difficulty of imitation, and irreplaceability.[19] According to RBT, companies are heterogeneous bundles of tangible resources (e.g., factories, cash reserves) and intangible resources (e.g., patents, brand loyalty) that must be combined strategically to exploit market opportunities.[20] RBT defines resources as various elements and combinations of elements that companies own or control to achieve their goals of providing products or services to society. Company resources include all inputs that enable the company to operate and implement its strategies.[21] These resources can be tangible or intangible, and

[18] Wernerfelt, B. (1984). A resource-based view of the firm. *Journal of Strategic Management*, 5(2), 171–180. https://doi.org/10.1002/smj.4250050207

[19] Barney, J. (1991). Enterprise resources and sustainable competitive advantage. *Journal of Management*, 17(1), 99–120. http://dx.doi.org/10.1177/014920639101700108

[20] Wernerfelt, B. (1984), A resource-based view of the firm. *Strategic Management Journal*, 5(2), 171–180._https://doi.org/10.1002/smj.4250050207

[21] Olavarrieta, S. (2014). Market attractiveness, resource-based and evolutionary approaches to strategy: A comparison. In Academy of Marketing Science: *Proceedings of the 1996 Academy of Marketing Science (AMS) Annual Conference* (pp. 149–153). Springer International Publishing. https://doi.org/10.1007/978-3-319-13144-3_41

they can be developed within the company or acquired on the market.[22] Tangible resources are physical assets that can be easily quantified, such as machinery, equipment, buildings, and financial resources. In contrast, intangible resources consist of non-physical assets that represent strategic value for the company, such as intellectual property, brand value, customer relationships, corporate culture, and employee skills and knowledge.

The effective management and use of both tangible and intangible resources is essential for companies seeking to achieve a sustainable competitive advantage in their respective markets. RBT emphasizes the value, scarcity, inimitability, and non-substitutability of resources. These characteristics are key to enabling resources to become a source of competitive advantage for companies. The theory emphasizes that the unique combination and effective management of resources can be an important differentiator for companies, creating the conditions for long-term success and sustainability in the market. Resource allocation, utilization, and management are important aspects of RBT in practice. Companies must fully exploit the potential of resources and realize their competitive advantages through effective allocation and utilization of resources as well as scientific management.

In relation to offshoring, RBT emphasizes the strategic use of a company's internal resources and capabilities to determine the optimal location for various business functions, with a focus on resource utilization and cost efficiency across international borders. The costs and acquisition of new skills are the main drivers of offshoring. However, a policy has emerged that prioritizes strategic factors such as increasing flexibility, seeking drivers of innovation, accessing global markets, and implementing organizational changes. In many industries, only globally competitive companies can hope to achieve a sustainable competitive advantage over their competitors.

According to RBT, companies analyze their unique resource base, including intellectual capital, technical expertise, and brand reputation, to assess which functions are best suited for offshore outsourcing. By identifying activities that are not part of their core business and do not contribute significantly to their competitive advantage, companies can reduce costs and shift resources to more strategic tasks. In addition, the decision-making process surrounding offshore outsourcing is influenced

[22] Hall, R. (2009). The strategic analysis of intangible resources. *Strategic Management Journal*, 13(2), 135–144.

by results-oriented budgeting methods. This approach takes into account the availability and potential benefits of additional resources in the foreign market, such as local partnerships, supply chain efficiency, and market knowledge.

RBT emphasizes the importance of aligning offshore outsourcing decisions with the internal capabilities of companies and the external resource landscape to ensure that these strategies not only reduce costs but also improve their overall strategic positioning in the global market. This careful alignment can lead to a more sustainable competitive advantage in an increasingly connected world. For example, a tech company may move software development to a country with a large pool of skilled programmers and employ professional workers to improve its product offering. Similarly, manufacturing companies may move production to regions with low labor costs and favorable trade agreements, optimizing their cost structure and improving profitability.

In addition, results-oriented companies place great importance on effectively managing the various risks associated with offshoring strategies. These risks include cultural differences that can lead to misunderstandings or miscommunication, regulation compliance difficulties resulting from different rules and legal requirements, and potential disruptions within the supply chain that can affect production times and operational efficiency. India, in particular, has proven to be an extremely attractive destination for US companies looking to move their operations overseas. One of the key factors contributing to this attractiveness is the fact that a significant portion of the Indian workforce speaks English, which greatly facilitates communication and collaboration between teams around the world. In addition, India's world-class institutions, such as the Indian Institutes of Technology, are ranked among the top 200 in the world, with specialized STEM programs that attract multinational R&D investments.[23] Mastercard is a good example. Mastercard, a globally renowned payments tech company, has implemented a "nearshoring" strategy in Central America in recent years, focusing on El Salvador and Costa Rica. With a 92% bilingual workforce and fintech-friendly regulations, Mastercard has successfully leveraged local resources and achieved significant development advantages. These countries have relatively cheap labor and

[23] Kimberly, A. (2022, June 16). How outsourcing jobs is affecting the US economy. https://www.thebalancemoney.com/how-outsourcing-jobs-affects-the-u-s-economy-3306279#citation-1

good infrastructure, which makes them an ideal environment for Mastercard to outsource its activities. Mastercard has established several service centers in Central America to provide services such as payment processing, customer service, and technical support to local and global customers. These service centers are not only cost-effective for Mastercard but also improve service quality and response times. Due to Central America's geographic proximity to the United States, time differences are less significant, enabling Mastercard to provide timely and efficient service to its customers. In addition, by working with the local government, Mastercard has obtained tax breaks and other incentives that further reduce its operating costs. These measures not only support Mastercard's business development in Central America but also promote local economic growth and job creation. Under El Salvador's Innovation Industry Incentives Act (2021), qualifying tech companies receive a 50% income tax reduction, a measure Mastercard reportedly used to reduce its operating costs by 18%.

Companies must conduct a comprehensive and careful assessment of the potential impact that various factors may have on their resource base. This assessment is essential because it helps them formulate effective outsourcing strategies to mitigate the associated risks while maximizing the potential benefits. Numerous researchers argue that the most important step toward outsourcing is defining the company's core competencies and the value it produces for consumers.[24] Jennings identifies several fundamental elements for a successful outsourcing strategy.[25]

(1) What are the objectives and where do they fit into the overall strategy? (2) Which activities should be outsourced? (3) Selection of suppliers. (4) Contract negotiations. (5) Transfer of activities and functions from the outsourcer to the supplier. (6) Choice of the relationship to be established with the supplier. There are several theoretical approaches that come into play when making offshore outsourcing decisions. While the RBV focuses on the use of complementary foreign resources, TCE evaluates the governance risks associated with cross-border operations. In short, RBT provides a framework for companies' offshore outsourcing decisions and enables them to optimize their resource allocation across

[24] Pellicelli, M. (2018). Gaining flexibility and innovation through offshore outsourcing. *Sustainability*, 10(5), 1672. https://doi.org/https://doi.org/10.3390/su10051672

[25] Jennings, D. (1996). Outsourcing opportunities for financial services. *Long Range Planning*, 29(3), 393–404. https://doi.org/10.1016/0024-6301(96)00025-8

international borders. By leveraging the complementary resources available in foreign markets, such as specialized skills, cost advantages, or unique technological innovations, companies can not only increase their operational efficiency but also significantly improve their competitive position in an increasingly globalized market. In addition, by proactively managing the risks associated with offshoring, such as cultural differences and regulatory challenges, companies can build a more resilient organizational structure. In this way, they can contribute to and promote the sustainable growth of the global economy by supporting innovation and mutually beneficial relationships across borders.

Based on the above theoretical analysis above, the relocation of US manufacturing to China has achieved a double benefit: cost savings and resource utilization. By moving production facilities to China, multinational companies can better respond to international demand and market changes, thereby strengthening their long-term growth and sustainability. Since the 1980s, the United States has experienced significant technological advances in telecommunications and computer technology. These changes resulted from high-tech competition with the Soviet Union and quickly spread from the military to the civilian sector. The low-cost, high-quality transfer of information has facilitated the expansion and intensification of offshore outsourcing with the aim of achieving the highest profits worldwide. Although the new wealthy Asian tigers have lost their attractiveness to US companies in terms of labor costs, China has emerged as an ideal partner to promote the global ambitions of American capitalists.

According to the book *Love and Trade War: China and the U.S. in Historical Context*, there are six main reasons for the shift of manufacturing from the United States to China: (1) outsourcing costs for US companies are significantly reduced, as the cost of Chinese workers is only 2% of the cost of US workers. In addition, wage levels can be kept extremely low for a long time, mainly because China has a seemingly endless supply of labor from its huge rural population. (2) Chinese workers are hardworking, eager to learn, and obedient. They are cheap but skilled workers in labor-intensive stages of production. (3) Access to China's abundant natural resources and large market reduces costs for US companies and increases their sales. (4) Environmental pollution is largely tolerated, poor working conditions are widely accepted, and troublesome independent unions are banned in Chinese factories. These cost-saving factors facilitate the influx of low-cost, acceptable-quality products into the United States. (5) The liberal offshoring policy of the United States fits perfectly with China's desire to accelerate its industrialization. The Chinese government grants US companies preferential treatment, ranging from free land leases to tax breaks and capital mobility. (6) The United States and China formed a military alliance against the Soviet Union and cooperated on most regional and global issues.[26] In addition, China is gradually transforming into a capitalist and more liberal country. All of these factors encourage US outsourcing to China. As a result, the share of manufacturing in US GDP declined from 21% in 1980 to 12% in 2007, while China became the world's second largest economy and the largest manufacturing nation three years later.[27]

In addition, India has become a base for outsourcing services. India is best known for its IT and BPO services. The BPO industry began to take shape in the late 1980s, represented by call centers, and saw significant growth in the 1990s with the liberalization and privatization of India in 1991. Since the early 2000s, the BPO industry has grown exponentially due to the commercialization of broadband Internet, making it easier to outsource more complex tasks and services overseas. During the same period, support from the Indian government accelerated the growth of the BPO industry. The BPO market, which gained a competitive advantage by merging small companies into large enterprises, was completed in 2004. As a result, India provided two thirds of all offshore IT services worldwide in 2005. The combined efforts of public and private institutions have created synergies and, thanks to high-speed Internet, Indian service exports have skyrocketed (Fig. 3.1).[28]

Production has become increasingly complex due to technological innovation,[29] and companies are now trying to manage this complexity through outsourcing. The advancing industrialization of some emerging

[26] Sheng, L., & do Nascimento, D. F. (2021). *Love and Trade War: China and the US in Historical Context*. Palgrave MacMillan.

[27] Botta, A. (2010). Economic development, structural change and booms in natural resources; A structuralist perspective. *Metroeconomica*, 61(3), 510–539. https://doi.org/10.1111/j.1467-999X.2009.04077.x

[28] Park, J. (2024). Outsourcing to India: The impact of service outsourcing to India on the US labor market. *Bulletin of Economic Research*, 76(1), 203–222. https://doi.org/10.1111/boer.12417

[29] Kang, M., Wu, X., Hong, P., & Park, Y. (2012). Aligning organizational control practices with competitive outsourcing performance. *Journal of Business Research*, 65(8), 1195–1201. https://doi.org/10.1016/j.jbusres.2011.07.004

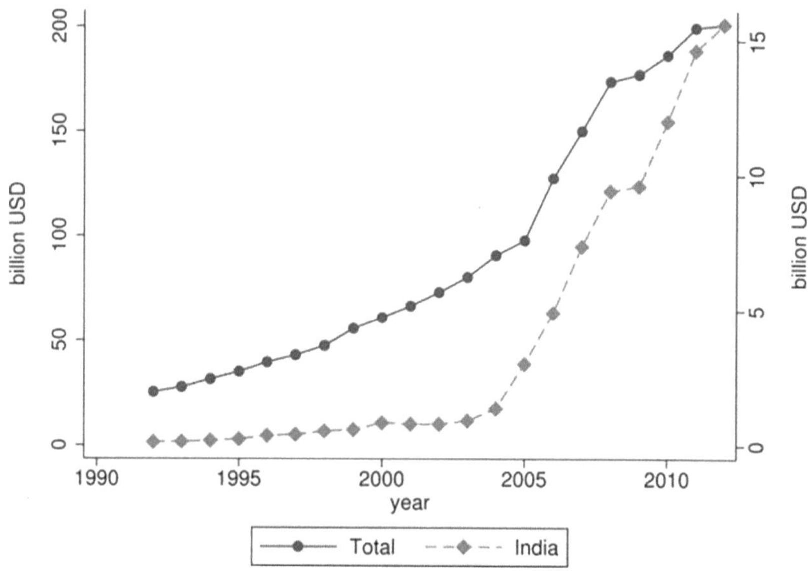

Fig. 3.1 Import of private services. *Source*: Park, J. (2024). Outsource to India: The impact of service outsourcing to India on the labor market in the United States. *Bulletin of Economic Research*, 76(1), 203–222

countries, such as China and India, has led to new forms of outsourcing, in which entire production functions are transferred to third parties. For these reasons, offshore outsourcing is changing the skills network. The search for new business models has also extended into new areas, from customer service to R&D, and even healthcare services. The pharmaceutical industry has seen a major development in outsourcing in new areas.[30]

[30] Van Arnum, P. (2008). Pharma ingredients—Outsourcing strategies of emerging pharmaceutical companies—Lessons for successful customer-supplier relationships. *Pharmaceutical Technology*, 32(10), 48.

3.2 The Social and Ecological Costs of Offshoring

As an economic activity in the context of globalization, offshoring brings many economic benefits, but inevitably also entails social costs. According to the World Bank's World Development Report 2021, the issue of offshore outsourcing has gained prominence in political and economic discourse. Specifically, 78% of OECD countries cite it as a policy priority.[31] Concerns about outsourcing are also prevalent in all areas of life. Interest in outsourcing exploded in 2004. That year, more than 1,000 references to the topic were found in four major newspapers, compared with fewer than 300 references in each of the previous two years. Discussions about outsourcing play an important role in popular culture, including jokes from late-night talk show hosts, numerous cartoons, and television shows such as CNN's Lou Dobbs Tonight Show.[32]

First, job losses are one of the notable social costs associated with offshoring. Studies show that Chinese exports to the United States have led to unemployment and hardship among manufacturing workers in certain areas, many of them rural.[33] According to the theory of comparative advantage, outsourcing usually occurs when the contracting country transfers production or service areas that do not have comparative advantages to the recipient country that does. In this process, some low-skilled or labor-intensive jobs in the contracting country may be replaced by workers from the recipient country, leading to a decline in employment in the corresponding industries in the contracting country. This job substitution effect is a direct effect of outsourcing on unemployment. Outsourcing is often accompanied by technological progress and industrial modernization. Through outsourcing, contracting countries can focus on production and service links with higher value added and promote technological innovation and industrial modernization.

[31] World Bank. (2021). World Development Report 2021: Data for better lives. https://openknowledge.worldbank.org/handle/10986/35218

[32] Mankiw, N. G., & Swagel, P. (2006). The politics and economics of offshore outsourcing. *Journal of Money*, 53(5), 1027–1056. https://doi.org/10.1016/j.jmoneco.2006.05.009

[33] Lai, E. L. C. (2019). The US-China trade war, US public opinion, and its impact on China. *Economic and Political Studies*, 7(2), 169–184. https://doi.org/10.1080/20954816.2019.1595330

However, this process can also lead to the disappearance of low-skilled jobs and an increase in high-skilled jobs, thereby changing the structure of employment. Workers who fail to adapt to such changes risk losing their jobs. In the short term, outsourcing can lead to job losses in certain industries in the host country, particularly low-skilled or labor-intensive jobs. In the long term, however, outsourcing can promote industrial upgrading and the optimization of the employment structure in the host country, thus creating more highly skilled jobs. For the host country, outsourcing can mean increased employment and economic growth. However, the impact of outsourcing on unemployment varies greatly depending on the industry. Some industries, such as manufacturing, are generally severely affected because low-skilled jobs are easily replaced. Others, such as the service sector, can benefit from the growth and job creation brought about by outsourcing. The skills and adaptability of workers are also key factors influencing the impact of outsourcing on unemployment. Workers with high skills and good adaptability are more likely to find new jobs in the changing employment structure caused by outsourcing. In contrast, low-skilled or less adaptable workers are at greater risk of unemployment.

Rising imports from China lead to higher unemployment, lower labor force participation, and lower wages in local labor markets where manufacturing industries competing with imports are located.[34] When companies relocate their operations to other countries or regions—usually in search of lower labor costs and greater efficiency—this often leads to a direct and often significant decline in employment opportunities in their home countries. This phenomenon is particularly pronounced in labor-intensive industries such as manufacturing and textiles, where the demand for low wages prompts companies to seek markets abroad. This can lead to sudden unemployment of many skilled and unskilled workers.

In the United States, job outsourcing occurs when US companies hire foreign workers instead of Americans. In 2019, US subsidiaries overseas employed 14.6 million workers abroad.[35] This affected not only the workers directly involved in the work in question but also affected

[34] Author, D. H., Dorn, D., & Hanson, G. H. (2013). The China syndrome: Local labor market effects of import competition in the United States. *American Economic Review*, 103(6), 2121–2168. https://www.aeaweb.org/articles?id=10.1257/aer.103.6.2121

[35] Bureau of Economic Analysis. (2021, November 12). Activities of US multinational enterprises: 2019.

employment in upstream and downstream industries, leading to higher unemployment and greater social instability. The most comprehensive cross-country analyses to date have been conducted by the OECD (2007) and Hijzen and Swaim (2007).[36] These studies use the share of value added in turnover by sector as a measure of outsourcing and link this indicator to job creation. This method is similar to that of Amiti and Wei (2005) but is adapted to the analysis of sector-specific data from 12 OECD countries (i.e., Austria, Belgium, Denmark, Finland, France, Germany, Greece, Italy, the Republic of Korea, Norway, Sweden, and the United States), covering 26 industries and a period from 1995 to 2000. The empirical results show that offshore outsourcing destroys jobs, albeit to a limited extent. A 1% increase in offshore outsourcing leads to a 0.15% decline in sectoral employment in manufacturing and a 0.08% decline in the service sector. In both cases, these are only direct effects.

In addition to manufacturing, outsourcing of services has an impact on employment. The import of services into the United States has increased significantly since the 1980s thanks to the development of communications technology. In the interest of reducing costs, relatively low-income countries and large English-speaking populations have become popular outsourcing hubs. These countries include India, Ireland, the Philippines, China, Malaysia, and some Eastern European countries.[37] Although offshoring of services may harm employment to some extent due to the displacement effect, it has a limited or even positive impact on employment because offshoring improves companies' productivity and reorganizes the composition of the workforce and tasks. Research suggests that as outsourcing increases, companies may need workers complementary to outsourced tasks, even within the same occupational group.[38] The tabloid press has largely blamed this practice for the loss of jobs in the service sector, suggesting that Americans are collectively opposed to

[36] Görg, H. (2011). Globalization, offshoring, and jobs. *Shaping Globalization in a Socially Sustainable Way*. Kiel Institute of World Economy Discussion Paper.

[37] Amiti, M., & Wei, S. J. (2005). The fear of outsourcing services: Is it justified? *Economic Policy*, 20(42), 308–347. https://doi.org/10.1111/j.1468-0327.2005.00140.x

[38] Park, J. (2024). Outsourcing to India: The effects of service outsourcing to India on the US labor market. *Bulletin of Economic Research*, 76(1), 203–222. https://doi.org/10.1111/boer.12417

the offshoring of professional services, a practice that leads to bankruptcies, divorces, and declining suburban property values because it inevitably leads to home foreclosures.[39]

However, it is important to emphasize that the growing income gap is a major problem that deserves attention. The theory of labor market segmentation explains the impact of outsourcing on income inequality. It states that labor markets are segmented rather than perfectly competitive, with barriers between workers of different skill levels and in different industries, leading to persistent wage differences and unequal opportunities. In outsourcing, the contracting country may relocate certain industries or branches of production to the recipient country, leading to a decrease in employment opportunities in these industries or branches. Low-skilled workers may face increased pressure on employment and the risk of lower wages. Conversely, highly skilled workers may benefit from more employment opportunities and higher wages due to industrial modernization and technological progress brought about by outsourcing.[40] This phenomenon of labor market segmentation contributes to the widening of income disparities.

Technological progress is a factor that cannot be ignored in the outsourcing process. Outsourcing often goes hand in hand with technology transfer and improvement, which can have a profound impact on labor markets in both client and contractor countries. For the recipient country, outsourcing may lead to automation or the relocation of low-skilled jobs to the recipient country, while high-skilled jobs may benefit from more opportunities due to technological progress. This change leads to an increase in the skill premium, so that the wage level of highly skilled workers increases relative to that of low-skilled workers. This phenomenon of rising skill premiums is known in economics as "skill-biased technological progress." For example, a 2022 OECD study shows that automation associated with outsourcing increases the skill premium in advanced economies by 8% to 12%. When providing outsourced services, the host country can also improve the qualifications and productivity of its workforce as a result of technological progress.

[39] Koku, P. S. (2015). A view from the street: An exploratory study of consumer attitudes toward offshoring of professional services in the United States. *Journal of Service Marketing*, 29(2), 150–159.

[40] Feenstra, R. C., & Hanson, G. H. (1996). Globalization, outsourcing, and wage inequality. *American Economic Review*, 86(2), 240–245.

However, as the countries concerned are usually at a lower stage of economic development, their labor market may be more dependent on low-skilled workers. As a result, the income gap between low- and high-skilled workers is likely to widen further, even if technological progress leads to higher overall wages. The principle of factor price equalization in international trade theory states that, under free trade conditions, factor prices tend to be the same in all countries. This principle can be called into question to some extent when it comes to outsourcing. First, outsourcing may lead to changes in the structure of trade between the contracting country and the country executing the contract. The contracting country may import more low-skilled and labor-intensive products while exporting high-skilled and labor-intensive products. This change in the trade structure may widen the income gap between the two countries.[41] Second, outsourcing can lead to segmentation and imperfect competition in factor markets. In the contracting country, the relative price of low-skilled labor may fall due to a fall in demand; in the host country, the relative price of low-skilled labor may rise due to increased demand. This change in factor prices may further exacerbate the rise in income inequality.

Although offshoring has improved the lifestyle and wages of the majority of US citizens, it has reduced the real wages of low-skilled workers in the US manufacturing sector.[42] Empirical studies show that two thirds of workers displaced by offshoring earned less after finding new jobs, with nearly 25% experiencing wage losses of 30% or more.[43] As a result, this widens the wage gap in the United States between low-skilled and high-skilled workers. Offshoring practices tend to favor the retention of highly skilled and well-paid positions, often found in sectors such as technology, finance, and management. These positions typically require advanced education and specialized training, giving companies a competitive advantage and allowing them to retain their most valuable employees. Conversely, low-skilled, low-income jobs, often found in

[41] Gu, X.H. & Sheng, L. (2010) A sensible tool for Pareto-improvement: Capital Controls. Journal of World Trade, 44(3), 567–590.

[42] Fennell, H. D. (2007). The significance of outsourcing and offshoring in the United States. University of Tennessee – Knoxville Dissertation.

[43] Marchant, M. A., & Kumar, S. (2005). An overview of foreign direct investment and outsourcing in the US. *Review of Agricultural Economics*, 27(3), 379–386. http://www.jstor.org/stable/3700863

manufacturing and services, are more susceptible to outsourcing to countries where labor costs are significantly lower. This trend not only leads to the displacement of many workers in industrialized countries but also exacerbates income inequality within society. As a result, the gap between the wealthy and the economically disadvantaged is widening, leading to greater social stratification.

Empirical analyses suggest that international outsourcing appears to have a more negative impact on wages in destination countries than other forms of offshoring; offshoring tends to benefit highly skilled workers and harm low-skilled workers, particularly in source countries.[44] Between 1970 and 2014, the share of middle-income households in all US households fell by 11% (from 58 to 47%). In other words, while middle-income families become richer or poorer, the income distribution in the United States has become polarized or widened.[45] This erosion reflects profound structural changes in the economy, where opportunities for stable, middle-income jobs are declining. Therefore, the impact of offshore outsourcing on overall revenue and economic health should not be underestimated.

In addition, offshoring can lead to the hollowing out of industries. The term "hollowing out" refers to the gradual weakening of an industry's status and function in the local economic system due to the loss of core elements such as resources, technology, and talent, which may lead to structural gaps in industrial capacity. Industrial life cycle theory suggests that every industry experiences cyclical changes, from birth to growth and from maturity to decline. In outsourcing, some industries may enter the decline phase prematurely due to factors such as technology transfer and changes in market demand, leading to a break in the industrial chain and the hollowing out of these industries.

This theory states that different countries or regions have different endowments of resources, technologies, talents, and other factors that determine their position and role in the global industrial chain. With the development of outsourcing, some countries or regions may be gradually pushed to the margins of the industrial chain due to the loss of key elements, leading to the hollowing out of their industries. If a large

[44] Cardoso, M., Neves, P. C., Afonso, O., & Sochirca, E. (2021). The impact of offshoring on wages: A meta-analysis. *Review of World Economics*, 157, 149–179. https://doi.org/10.1007/s10290-020-00385-z

[45] Rishav, T. (2024, June 20). What is hollowing out? WSO.

number of companies decide to outsource their core business functions or production processes to countries with lower labor costs, the corresponding industries in the domestic market are likely to gradually shrink. This trend can lead to an unbalanced industrial structure in which certain sectors become overly dependent on foreign labor, while local skills are neglected. The consequences of this shift pose a potential threat to a country's long-term economic development and its ability to improve its industrial base. As industries shrink and local expertise declines, the country's economic autonomy may be weakened, making it more vulnerable to global market fluctuations and external shocks. Furthermore, lower local production can hinder innovation and technological progress, as companies lose the incentive to invest in R&D. This erosion of industrial resilience can have far-reaching consequences and jeopardize the country's economic stability and growth prospects.

At the capital market level, outsourcing also contributes to a loss of security in the economy. Outsourcing can lead to reduced local taxes and tax revenues. With the relocation of production or service relationships, taxes originally paid by local companies may gradually flow to the countries or regions where external suppliers are located, affecting the tax revenues and level of public services provided by local governments.[46] In outsourcing, companies relocate part of their production or service activities to other countries or regions, which is often accompanied by the repatriation of profits. Companies may be more inclined to send their profits to countries or regions where outsourcing is practiced because they offer more favorable tax policies or lower labor costs. This profit repatriation behavior leads directly to the loss of domestic capital. In addition, outsourcing may cause companies to transfer some of their assets or funds to other countries or regions to avoid risks or seek better investment opportunities. This transfer of assets or funds further exacerbates the problem of capital flight from the home country.

In outsourcing, companies may be exposed to exchange rate risk. Fluctuations in exchange rates in different countries or regions can cause losses for companies. To avoid this risk, companies may be more inclined to transfer funds to countries or regions with relatively stable exchange rates. Such transfers further exacerbate the problem of capital outflows

[46] Slemrod, J., & Wilson, J. D. (2009). Tax competition with parasitic tax havens. *Journal of Public Economics*, 93(11–12), 1261–1270. https://doi.org/10.1016/j.jpubeco.2009.06.004

from the country. As companies increasingly engage in offshoring, this may lead to increased tax asymmetry, whereby certain companies take advantage of lower tax jurisdictions to minimize the amount of tax they pay. This practice not only leads to capital outflows that drain vital financial resources from national economies but also creates numerous threats to the economic security of individual states and the global economy as a whole.[47] Such capital flight can undermine the financial stability of states and lead to a drop in government revenues, which are essential for financing public services and infrastructure projects.

Outsourcing not only leads to lower tax revenues but can also increase pressure on government spending. With the popularity of outsourcing, some goods or services that were originally provided by domestic companies may gradually be replaced by external providers. This can lead to a decline in the competitiveness of domestic companies in the international market, which in turn affects their profitability. To ensure the survival and development of companies, the government may need to provide more financial support and subsidies.

Furthermore, outsourcing can lead to increased unemployment and labor market volatility. To alleviate pressure on employment and maintain social stability, the government may have to increase spending on unemployment benefits and workforce training. These additional expenses further exacerbate fiscal pressures on the government and leads to a drop in tax revenues. In addition, the growing burden of social welfare is a social cost factor that cannot be ignored. The hollowing out of industries often leads to a vicious cycle: loss of housing, loss of pensions, reduction of the local tax base, reduction of local public services, loss of local institutional resources, and physical deterioration of cities.

Furthermore, the hollowing out of industries in the United States almost always means a loss of health benefits for workers, as health care in the United States is often tied to employment. In this case, the state must adapt by assuming more social costs. Rising unemployment means increased pressure on the social security system, and governments have to spend more on benefits such as unemployment benefits and retraining, further increasing the financial burden.

High unemployment also affects social stability and security. For example, as unemployment rises and living conditions deteriorate, crime

[47] Hobela, V. (2020). Economic offshoring in national economic security. *Scientific Horizons*, 23(12), 109–120.

rates increase, conflict and violence arise, people suffer from physical and mental health problems, and depression rates rise. This affects people's satisfaction and sense of security and also increases the costs of maintaining social stability, as more police and security forces are needed, more investment is required in medical resources, and medical security expenditures rise.

The United States frequently resorts to punitive measures in response to social unrest and crime caused by industrialization, leading to a significant difference in life expectancy between the poor and the rich and further exacerbating social inequality. Between 2001 and 2014, deindustrialization and incarceration were significant factors in the life expectancy of the poor, but not the rich, leading to significant health deficits in states that responded to economic stagnation with punishment.[48]

The political response to this form of social unrest has been largely punitive, as evidenced by the gradual expansion of the penal state and the elimination of social welfare in recent decades. This further perpetuates and exacerbates inequalities in life expectancy. The impact of outsourcing on working conditions and the working environment is also important. As outsourcing is often associated with low-skilled and high-intensity work, it can lead to problems such as poor working conditions and a poor working environment in the host country. This can have a negative impact on the protection of workers' rights and social stability in the host country. At the same time, offshoring poses challenges related to cultural and social integration. When companies engage in offshoring, they can trigger cultural conflicts and value differences between different countries and regions. These differences can have profound effects on social harmony and stability, as different cultural norms and business practices can lead to misunderstandings and friction between teams.

Offshoring usually involves collaboration between different countries and regions, and language barriers are one of the main challenges of offshore collaboration. For example, English is not the official or common language in all outsourcing destination countries, which can lead to misinterpretations and delays in the transmission of information. In addition

[48] Nosrati, E., Ash, M., Marmot, M., McKee, M., & King, L. P. (2018). The association between income and life expectancy revisited: deindustrialization, incarceration and the widening health gap. *International Journal of Epidemiology*, 47(3), 720–730. https://doi.org/10.1093/ije/dyx243

to language itself, there are cultural differences in nonverbal communication methods, such as body language, facial expressions, and tone of voice. These differences can lead to misunderstandings and conflicts in communication.

Differences in cultural values and work ethics exacerbate these challenges. For example, some cultures place a high value on teamwork and collectivism, while others emphasize individualism and competition. These differences can lead to friction and misunderstandings in the workplace. Differences in perception of time and work pace can also affect the smooth running of a project. For example, some cultures are accustomed to a fast pace of work, while others place more value on job stability and sustainability. The psychosocial effects of offshoring include employee alienation from the corporate culture, reduced work motivation, and reduced organizational commitment. This feeling of alienation can affect employee motivation and loyalty. Geographically dispersed teamwork can also lead to a weakened sense of social identity and belonging among employees, as team members may come from different cultures and regions. In some outsourcing destinations, labor laws may not be perfect, and the rights and interests of workers may not be fully protected. This may lead to u Trade Balance ir treatment or the loss of rights and interests in the employees' work. Cross-border labor deployment can also involve legal issues such as visas and work permits, which can increase labor costs and legal risks for companies.

Cultural differences and social integration problems can trigger social conflicts and destabilizing factors. For example, cultural differences can lead to misunderstandings and conflicts among team members, which in turn hinders the smooth running of the project. According to previous research, cultural differences may affect factors critical to offshore outsourcing success, namely relationship quality (e.g., trust, supplier performance, cooperation, and conflict).[49] When teams from different backgrounds work together, misunderstandings and differing expectations can lead to tensions and hinder cooperation. For example, a random

[49] Winkler, J. K., Dibbern, J., & Heinzl, A. (2008). The impact of cultural differences in offshore outsourcing – Case study results from German-Indian application development projects. *Information Systems Frontiers*, 10, 243–258. https://doi.org/10.1007/s10796-008-9068-5

sample of 60 executives involved in IT offshoring cited "cultural differences" as the most important "major problem" in offshoring.[50] Similarly, Lewin et al. (2005) survey 96 US companies that have outsourced their services abroad or are planning to do so. They find that the most frequently cited "risk in moving work abroad" is "service quality" (59%), followed by "cultural fit" (58%).[51]

Overall, the social costs of offshoring are multifaceted and complex. To effectively mitigate these negative effects, governments and businesses must work together. Governments should play an active role in formulating relevant policies that address the complex aspects of offshoring and ensure that they support the workers affected. This includes strengthening training and retraining initiatives to equip workers with the skills needed for new labor markets. In addition, they should promote industrial modernization and innovation to create more quality employment opportunities. Furthermore, companies seeking economic benefits and competitive advantages through offshoring must recognize and accept their social responsibility. This means that they must be aware of the long-term impact of their outsourcing decisions on local communities and society at large. By promoting a culture of corporate social responsibility, companies can contribute to a more sustainable economic environment in which profit motives and social justice are balanced.

The effects of offshoring are not limited to economic and social aspects; environmental problems also require people's vigilance. As an important economic phenomenon, global outsourcing has developed rapidly since the mid-1990s and has become the main trend in a new round of global industrial transfer. However, with the increase in outsourcing activities, environmental pollution and ecological damage have also become increasingly prominent, with significant implications for human health.

Cross-border transfer of environmental costs is a systemic feature of today's global value chains. By shifting environmentally harmful production to developing countries, the United States has not only relocated

[50] Metters, R. (2008). A case study of national culture and offshoring services. *International Journal of Operations & Production Management*, 28(8), 727–747. https://doi.org/10.1108/01443570810888616

[51] Lewin, A., Peacock, M., Peeters, C., Russell, J., & Sutton, G. (2005). *Results of the 2nd Semi-annual Offshore Survey, December 2005*. Duke University CIBER/Archstone Consulting.

jobs but also systematically externalized environmental burdens, thereby creating a paradigm of "unequal ecological exchange." This paradigm is reflected in two dimensions. While the United States generates "clean GDP" through imports of industrial products, more than 85% of the associated emissions are absorbed by outsourcing countries such as China. At the same time, export-oriented growth is forcing developing countries to overexploit their ecological capital, as demonstrated by the 300% increase in deforestation rates in Southeast Asia to meet US demand for timber. This dual mechanism of exploitation—a combination of environmental and labor oppression—leads to a balance of "low wages and high pollution" in offshore hubs such as Bangladesh. These findings show how US economic hegemony goes beyond financial dominance and leads to institutionalized ecological displacement through international trade regimes.[52]

The offshoring process can lead to excessive resource consumption, causing significant environmental problems. In outsourcing, the efficiency of resource utilization is often low due to information asymmetry between the external provider and the company, as well as the provider's pursuit of short-term profit maximization. The problem of excessive resource consumption is often not effectively curbed due to a lack of or inadequate monitoring mechanisms. When companies relocate their production or services to distant regions, the associated logistics often require the transport of large quantities of materials. This transport of goods undeniably leads to higher energy consumption and carbon emissions. For example, transporting raw materials and finished products over long distances between different countries not only involves the combustion of large quantities of fossil fuels but also contributes to the release of significant amounts of greenhouse gases. These emissions have a negative impact on the global climate and exacerbate problems such as climate change and air pollution.

To successfully take over industries, the relocation of production sites can lead to a reduction in environmental standards. The pollution haven hypothesis (PHH) states that strict US regulations and institutional pressure on environmental performance may be detrimental to the environment in other countries due to the offshoring strategy of US

[52] Rice, J. (2007). Ecologically unequal exchange: International trade and unequal use of ecological space in the world system. *Social Forces*, 85(3), 1369–1392.

companies.[53] According to the PHH, "liberalized trade in goods will lead to a shift in environmentally intensive production from high-income countries with strict environmental regulations to low-income countries with lax environmental regulations."

Regions where offshoring is practiced may have relatively lax environmental regulations and controls. This allows companies to use more environmentally harmful production methods, which can cause serious damage to the local ecosystem. For example, certain regions have few restrictions on wastewater discharge and emissions, which can lead to deterioration of water resources and air quality. The relocation of certain industries can encroach on original natural habitats and disrupt the local ecological balance. The construction of new factories or plants can lead to deforestation and the destruction of wetlands, threatening the habitat of local plants and animals. Take the example of Union Carbide India Limited (UCIL), an outsourced chemical company founded by Union Carbide Corporation in India and based in Bhopal, Madhya Pradesh, India. In the early hours of December 3, 1984, a toxic gas leak at the UCIL plant shocked the world and became a classic example of an outsourcing company damaging the environment due to lax local environmental standards. *The New York Times*, *Time Magazine*, and local Indian media reported that the UCIL plant used methyl isocyanate (MIC), a highly toxic chemical, in the production of pesticides. Due to the factory's outdated safety equipment and relatively lax environmental standards in India at the time, UCIL did not implement adequate safety management and storage of hazardous substances such as MIC. On December 3, 1984, due to mistakes made by workers, a large quantity of MIC gas was released and quickly spread in and around the city of Bhopal. The leak caused at least 5,000 immediate deaths, hundreds of thousands of injuries, and long-term health effects for millions more. MIC gas not only caused acute poisoning and deaths but also triggered long-term environmental pollution and health problems, such as respiratory diseases, neurological disorders, and skin diseases.

Waste disposal is also an important issue. Waste generated by offshoring may be improperly disposed of during transportation and disposal between different regions, further exacerbating environmental

[53] Li, X., & Zhou, Y. M. (2017). Offshoring environmental pollution while shifting production? *Strategic Management Journal*, 38(11), 2310–2329. https://doi.org/10.1002/smj.2656

pollution. For example, a study conducted in China using atmospheric models finds that 17% to 36% of the four most significant anthropogenic air pollutants (i.e., sulfur dioxide, nitrogen oxide, carbon monoxide, and black carbon) emitted in that country are linked to the production of goods for export, and that about 21% of export-related emissions are attributable to goods destined for the United States.[54] This highlights the global nature of the waste and emissions problem and shows how industrial practices in one country can have far-reaching environmental consequences in another. Improper waste disposal not only harms local ecosystems but also contributes to broader problems such as climate change and deteriorating air quality.

A prominent case study of environmental damage caused by corporate outsourcing in host countries concerns Royal Dutch Shell's oil extraction activities in the Niger Delta in Nigeria.[55] As one of the world's largest energy companies, Shell has been operating vast oil extraction facilities in Nigeria since 1958, with devastating consequences for the local environment. According to relevant reports and statistics, Shell has frequently spilled oil in Nigeria, causing significant pollution of large areas of land and water sources. These oil spills not only destroy the local ecosystem but also pose a major threat to the lives and health of local residents.

Specifically, independent reports document frequent oil spills from Shell's Nigerian operations, which have contaminated more than 11,000 square kilometers of land and water. In the 2008 Bodo oil spill, approximately 4,000 barrels of oil were released, contaminating 35 square kilometers of mangrove ecosystems.[56] The oil quickly spread to local rivers, lakes, and agricultural land, deteriorating water quality, contaminating soil, and reducing crop yields. Due to the lack of clean water and food, the health of local residents has deteriorated significantly, and the incidence of skin diseases, respiratory diseases, and other illnesses has increased considerably.

[54] Lin, J., et. al. (2014). China's international trade and air pollution in the United States. *Proceedings of the National Academy of Sciences*, 111(5), 1736–1741. https://doi.org/10.1073/pnas.1312860111

[55] Amnesty International. (2021). Neglect in the Niger Delta. https://www.amnesty.org/en/documents/afr44/4010/2021/

[56] Fentiman, A., & Zabbey, N. (2015). Environmental degradation and cultural erosion. *Oryx*, 49(4), 581–591.

In addition to direct oil pollution, Shell's extraction activities result in significant greenhouse gas emissions. These emissions not only exacerbate the problem of global climate change but also have negative impacts on the local climate and environment in Nigeria. For example, greenhouse gas emissions have led to increased local temperatures and decreased rainfall, further exacerbating the problems of drought and desertification.

Shell's mining activities in Nigeria have sparked widespread social controversy and protests. Local residents and environmental groups have accused Shell of environmental damage and pollution and demanded that the company take responsibility. However, Shell often shirks its responsibility for various reasons and even tries to cover up the fact that it causes environmental damage. This case reminds us once again that companies must not only aim for economic gains but also assume the corresponding social and environmental responsibility. In the long term, the environmental costs of offshoring can threaten the stability and sustainability of the global ecosystem. This affects the quality of life of the current generation and poses a potential risk to the survival and development of future generations. Several proactive measures can be taken to mitigate these risks. First, companies can adopt more sustainable practices by investing in greener technologies and sourcing materials responsibly. Second, governments can adopt stricter regulations on waste disposal and emissions to ensure that companies are held accountable for their environmental footprint. Finally, promoting international cooperation on environmental standards can help create a unified approach to sustainability in global trade.

CHAPTER 4

A Global Economy for the Future

4.1 Introduction

In today's globalized and interconnected economic system, global imbalances are growing, making the current growth pattern worryingly abnormal. From an economic perspective, major imbalances in global trade constitute one of the biggest problems. This abnormal trade pattern has distorted global resource allocation and led to an over-reliance on foreign demand to fuel growth, while other countries suffer from deindustrialization, rising unemployment, and reduced resilience. In terms of industrial structure, the irrational global division of labor further exacerbates the distortion of growth patterns. The misguided priorities of some countries, focusing too much on the financial sector and high value-added services while neglecting the development of the real economy, particularly the manufacturing sector, have made their economic structures vulnerable. Once the financial market fluctuates, the entire economic system may be affected and fall into crisis and instability. Regarding the distribution of resources, these are overly concentrated in a few industrialized countries and regions of the world, while the vast majority of developing countries suffer from a lack of resources. Neither the debt-driven growth model used by industrialized countries nor the export-driven growth strategy adopted by emerging economies are sustainable in the long term.

E. Li Sheng, *A Recent History of Global Imbalances*,
https://doi.org/10.1007/978-981-95-1834-0_4

To make matters worse, growing trade protectionism is hampering global trade liberalization and threatening economic coordination. Indeed, increasing trade protectionism and escalating trade conflicts not only hinder the liberalization and facilitation of global trade but also restrict trade between countries and pose a serious threat to the coordinated development of the global economy. In the face of these challenges, countries around the world must work together to overcome them and promote the healthy and sustainable development of the global economy.

The COVID-19 pandemic severely disrupted global value chains and highlighted the importance of industrial production autonomy in areas such as healthcare, food, and energy. In this context, the reindustrialization strategy, which aims to revitalize and strengthen a country's industrial sector, particularly by increasing production capacities, is especially important. In recent years, the US government has taken active steps to promote and support domestic production. It offers incentives for manufacturers to invest in new technologies and provides tax breaks by implementing various policy measures and initiatives. The strategic use of these policy measures and initiatives has triggered the development of various frameworks and initiatives designed to drive industrial growth and innovation. These policy measures often include strong support for domestic production to promote local industry and reduce dependence on imports. The revival of the manufacturing industry has attracted the attention of all countries, and the European Union and Russia have also made efforts to actively develop the manufacturing industry.

Geopolitical tensions and frequent disruptions to global value chains have forced policymakers to review and adapt their globalization strategies. In this context, the strategy of "friendly outsourcing" has gradually become a priority for many countries. The aim is to strengthen economic relations and cooperation with allies by reshaping international trade and supply chains to support each other in times of crisis. This model not only helps to reduce risks in the supply chain but also significantly improves industrial stability and security. At the same time, the "Indo-Pacific" strategy proposed by the United States as a new blueprint for regional development is leading to a rebalancing of power in the region between the United States and its partner countries. This strategy aims to strengthen alliances and partnerships, enhance military presence and capabilities, promote economic integration, and uphold shared values and interests.

There are two main reasons for this shift in strategic language, which will have a profound impact on the global landscape. First, geoeconomic factors cannot be ignored. With the recovery of the global economy, trade volumes have skyrocketed, particularly the long-distance transport of energy flows between the Indian Ocean and the Pacific Ocean. Second, geopolitical factors are equally crucial, particularly the rise of China, which has greatly influenced the regional landscape, while India still plays an important role despite its relatively minor influence in the region. Overall, the political and economic nature of the world is quietly evolving.

4.2 The Unsustainability of the Current Growth Model

In today's interconnected and globalized economic landscape, global imbalances have become increasingly pronounced in recent years, leading to a growth pattern characterized by significant and worrying divergences. In economic terms, the major problem is the persistent imbalance in global trade. Some industrialized countries have long-standing trade deficits, indicating that they import far more than they export, whereas emerging economies have accumulated substantial trade surpluses and benefit from their ability to produce goods at lower costs.

Although this may be a reasonable growth strategy for a country, especially if it is starting from a position of excessive external debt, it comes at the expense of other countries, and the problem can become systemic if several countries that represent a significant share of global trade pursue this strategy.[1] This unbalanced trade pattern has led to a distorted distribution of resources at the global level, with some countries relying heavily on foreign demand to fuel their economic growth. In contrast, other countries are facing the worrying consequences of deindustrialization, which often leads to job losses and reduced economic resilience.

In terms of industrial structure, the irrational division of labor at the global level has significantly exacerbated the deformation of the growth model. Since the second half of the twentieth century, the system of global industrial division of labor has undergone significant changes and transformations. However, with the deepening of the globalization

[1] Blanchard, O. J., & Milesi-Ferretti, G. M. (2010). Global imbalances: In the middle? Available at SSRN 1525542.

process, the irrationality and unsustainability of the global industrial division of labor have become increasingly evident. The global industrial division of labor refers to the specialized production and cooperation of industries and products by all countries in the world according to their own resource endowments, technological levels, and market conditions.

At present, the global industrial division of labor has the following characteristics:

Highly specialized and refined: With the advancement of science and technology and the deepening of the global market, the global industrial division of labor is increasingly moving toward high specialization and refinement. Depending on their own advantages, countries specialize in one or more areas and form different links in the global industrial chain.

Multinational corporations and global supply chains: Multinational corporations play an important role in the global division of industrial labor. Through global supply chains, they distribute production activities from various links around the world to minimize costs and maximize profits.

Increasing participation of developing countries: With the progress of globalization and economic integration, more and more developing countries are participating in the global division of industrial labor. They experienced rapid economic development by taking over industrial transfers from industrialized countries.

Over the past half-century, the global economy has experienced profound changes in the geographical distribution of industrial activities and in the structure of the international division of labor. These changes have been central elements of the so-called contemporary process of globalization. In this process, the consolidation of East Asia as a manufacturing center is crucial.[2] Ricardo's law of comparative advantage, which forms the basis of the current theory of the international division of labor, can be summarized as follows. The structure of international trade is based on the principle of comparative labor costs, which states that when two countries enter into trade relations and both produce the same goods,

[2] Grinberg, N. (2016). Global commodity chains and the production of value at the global level: The new theory of international division of labor is revived. *Journal of World-Systems Research*, 22(1), 247–278. https://doi.org/10.5195/jwsr.2016.605

one country will sell the goods for which its relative (rather than absolute) costs are lower, and the other country will sell the goods for which its own costs are lower.[3]

However, although the international division of labor has minimized costs and optimized economic benefits, it has led to imbalances in national economic structures and global trade imbalances. A number of countries have focused too much on high value-added sectors, such as the financial sector and various services, neglecting the crucial development of the real economy, particularly the manufacturing sector. This distorted prioritization has led to structural weaknesses in their economies. Volatility in financial markets can affect the entire economic system, making it vulnerable to crises and instability. Multinational companies have established global production systems based on labor-intensive export platforms in low-wage regions. This trend toward industrialization in the Third World and the decline of manufacturing as a share of GDP in the West and Japan are driven by the structural capitalist imperative of profit maximization under conditions of intensified global competition, often at the expense of domestic production capacities.[4]

Although the global division of labor has to some extent promoted the prosperity and development of the world economy, its irrationality has become increasingly evident. Resource endowment and division of labor are not compatible. Resource endowment is an important factor determining the division of labor in a country or region. However, in reality, there is often a mismatch between resource endowment and the industrial division of labor. Some countries are rich in natural resources but cannot fully exploit them due to limited technological levels, institutional environments, and other factors, leading to resource waste and inefficiency.

In contrast, although some countries are relatively lacking in natural resources, they can occupy an important position in the global industrial division of labor due to their advantages in technological innovation, human resources, and other aspects. However, this pattern of division of

[3] Mittelman, J. H. (1995). Rethinking the international division of labor in the context of globalization. *Third World Quarterly*, 16(2), 273–296. https://doi.org/10.1080/01436599550036130

[4] Mittelman, J. H. (1995). Rethinking the international division of labor in the context of globalization. *Third World Quarterly*, 16(2), 273–296. https://doi.org/10.1080/01436599550036130

labor often leads to an excessive concentration of resources in a few countries, exacerbating the unequal distribution of resources in the world. The division of labor in the global value chain is one of the most important features of the current global industrial division of labor.

However, the division of labor in global value chains is often characterized by inequalities. Industrialized countries occupy a dominant position in global value chains and control high value-added areas such as R&D, design, and marketing, while developing countries mainly take on low value-added areas such as processing and assembly. This type of division of labor gives developing countries a passive position in the global industrial chain and a lack of voice and bargaining power.

Industrialized countries have now succeeded in controlling and exploiting global industries by controlling the most important links in global value chains. The irrationality of the global industrial division of labor is also evident in environmental pollution and resource consumption. To attract foreign investment and carry out industrial transfers, some developing countries often neglect environmental and resource protection, leading to environmental pollution and excessive resource consumption. Furthermore, within the global industrial division of labor, multinational companies and global supply chains tend to pursue short-term profit maximization while ignoring long-term environmental impacts and resources.

In terms of resource distribution, global imbalances have led to an excessive concentration of resources. A few developed countries and regions have large amounts of capital, technology, and human resources, while the vast majority of developing countries face a lack of resources. Excessive resource concentration refers to the uneven distribution of resources around the world, meaning that resources are overly concentrated in some countries or regions while being relatively scarce in others. This concentration is evident in natural resources, capital, technology, and human resources.

Excessive concentration of natural resources: Some countries are rich in natural resources, such as oil, minerals, and agricultural products, while others lack them. This uneven distribution means that resource-rich countries have stronger bargaining power in the global market, while resource-poor countries face higher production costs.

Excessive concentration of capital: Capital circulates worldwide, but tends to be concentrated in a few developed countries or financial centers.

This concentration leads to an unequal distribution of capital between countries, exacerbating global imbalances.

Excessive concentration of technology: Technological innovations and advanced technologies tend to be concentrated in a few developed countries or industries. This concentration limits the diffusion and application of technology in developing countries and exacerbates the global technological imbalance.

Excessive concentration of human resources: High-quality talent tends to be concentrated in a few developed countries or cities. This concentration leads to brain drain from developing countries and exacerbates the global imbalance in human resources (Table 4.1).

Western economies (along with Japan) hold a disproportionate share of global wealth, especially human resources. "This international inequality acts as a form of conspicuous consumption, with less developed nations tending to try to emulate the more prosperous nations. The rich nations

Table 4.1 Wealth/capital per capita and components by region (1994) (in US dollars)

	Natural capital	*Human resources*	*Produced assets*	*Total wealth*
North America	15,429	247,892	61,953	325,274
Pacific OECD	7447	205,156	89,786	302,389
Western Europe	5604	175,570	54,990	236,164
Middle East	63,041	55,898	27,304	146,243
South America	8666	69,548	15,872	94,086
Eastern Europe, etc	10,714	30,530	22,256	62,500
North Africa	2803	37,034	14,348	54,185
Central America	3182	40,628	7801	51,612
East Asia	5046	35,207	7220	46,076
East/South Africa	2992	19,526	7345	29,863
South Asia	3622	13,959	4123	21,704

Source Dixon and Hamilton (1996, p. 16)

acquired their wealth through imperialism and later through hegemonic control of world resources via the market economy."[5] To reduce inequality, Africa and South Asia in particular must be able to challenge this hegemony by building social and human capital over a long period.

Differences such as income disparities, technological gaps, and industrial structures in the economic development of different countries, regions, or economies contribute significantly to global imbalances. Industrialized countries, with their advanced production technology, ability to use resources efficiently, and perfect market system, attract a large amount of capital and human resources, thus exacerbating the excessive concentration of resources. In contrast, developing countries often find it difficult to attract and efficiently use resources due to underdeveloped technological infrastructure, inadequate infrastructure networks, and institutional gaps.

Furthermore, factors such as unequal international trade and investment rules, asymmetric information, and differences in market power tend to cause resources to flow to countries and industries with competitive advantages. This unequal distribution of international trade and investment further exacerbates the excessive concentration of resources. For example, some industrialized countries occupy a dominant position in the global industrial chain by controlling key technologies and market channels, thus obtaining more resources and advantages. Institutional and political differences between countries, regions, or economies are also important factors leading to excessive concentration of resources. For example, some countries attract large amounts of capital and human resources through measures such as favorable tax policies and perfect infrastructure and public services, whereas other countries have imperfect institutional environments and weak policy implementation, making it difficult to attract and use resources effectively. These institutional and political differences further contribute to excessive concentration of resources and global imbalances.

This unequal distribution of resources has seriously hampered the concerted development of the global economy and perpetuated the problems of poverty and inequality on a global scale. The consequences of this imbalance are far-reaching, as developing countries struggle to access the tools necessary for growth and innovation, thereby widening the

[5] O'Hara, P. A. (2001). Wealth distribution and global inequality in the multiple capital paradigm. *International Journal of Human Development*, 1(1), 121–140.

economic divide. Furthermore, the concentration of resources in rich countries creates a cycle in which these nations continue to prosper while poorer countries remain trapped in a cycle of underdevelopment. This situation fundamentally undermines global efforts to achieve sustainable development and equitable growth.

From a theoretical perspective, the resource curse phenomenon represents a critical paradox. This refers to the fact that resource-rich countries often suffer from problems such as slow economic growth, political instability, and social conflict due to their excessive dependence on resource exports. The reason is that revenues from resource exports are often used for unproductive expenditures such as military spending, corruption, and rent-seeking, rather than being invested in long-term growth areas such as education, healthcare, and infrastructure. Excessive concentration of resources can also hinder technological innovation. Technological innovation is a key factor in promoting economic growth and industrial modernization, but excessive concentration of resources can lead to a lack of incentives and financial support for technological innovation. Indeed, technological innovation requires a good innovation environment and financial support.

However, if resources are overly concentrated, technological innovation can be hampered by obstacles such as a lack of money, brain drain, and institutional constraints. This may lead to a slowdown in technological innovation and undermine the competitiveness and sustainable development of the global economy. Excessive concentration of resources can also harm the ecological environment. The protection and sustainable development of the ecological environment are key to long-term economic growth and social prosperity. However, when resources are too concentrated, the ecological environment can be damaged by excessive exploitation and use, leading to ecosystem imbalance and loss of biodiversity. This may increase global climate change, the frequency of natural disasters, and the deterioration of the ecological environment.

The accumulation of debt in the global economy has become a problem that cannot be ignored. As debt levels rise, so do risks in the financial system. If a debt crisis were to erupt, it would have profound implications for economic growth. The causes of debt accumulation include government budget deficits, excessive corporate borrowing, and the expansion of consumer credit for private individuals. These debt problems can not only lead to instability in the financial system but also trigger a chain reaction with serious consequences for the entire economic system.

According to the latest IMF data, global government debt continues to rise. The total external debt of all low- and middle-income countries reached a record high of $8.8 trillion at the end of 2023, an increase of 8% from 2020. The total external debt of countries eligible for borrowing from the World Bank's International Development Association climbed to $1.1 trillion. At the same time, government debt in industrialized countries has reached alarming levels. For example, the US federal government's debt has exceeded the $35 trillion mark and now represents more than 120% of US GDP. The IMF estimates that global public debt could reach 100% of GDP by 2030, an increase of 10 percentage points from 2019.[6]

The impact of global debt problems on economic growth cannot be ignored. High debt levels limit governments' fiscal room for maneuver and make it more difficult for them to respond to future downturns or emergencies with massive new fiscal stimulus. This could lead to a slowdown in recovery and even trigger a new recession. In addition, high debt levels increase government financing costs, which in turn leads to an increase in the general level of interest rates. This will have a negative impact on financing for businesses and individuals and dampen investment and consumption, which in turn will slow economic growth.

High levels of debt can also trigger volatility in financial markets. As debt levels rise, investors become increasingly fearful of debt defaults, leading to greater instability in financial markets. At the same time, high interest rates increase the credit risk of financial institutions, which can trigger a financial crisis. As debt levels rise, governments must devote more funds to debt servicing, leading to corresponding cuts in development spending. For developing countries, this undermines their ability to finance essential public services such as health, education, and climate protection. For example, one third of developing countries spend more on debt interest than on programs in key areas of human development such as healthcare, education, and climate protection.

A debt-driven economy refers to a system in which modern economic growth increasingly depends on debt financing (i.e., the availability and flow of credit) rather than traditional asset-side factors. Unlike

[6] International Monetary Fund. (2023). *World Economic Outlook: Tackling Debt*. IMF.

conventional macroeconomic concepts, which focus on productive assets and production, a debt-driven economy emphasizes the crucial role of debt, credit, and financialization in shaping economic outcomes. As a post-Keynesian, Minsky was the first economist to address the fatal consequences of financing problems for the economy and to develop a systematic theory. According to him, the modern economy is a credit economy, namely a debt economy. By printing money and issuing bonds, it is possible to temporarily solve the problem of insufficient demand and even eliminate economic crises. However, debt is also a disease of civilization. When countries, companies, and individuals become dependent on debt, all sorts of side effects occur once a bubble bursts. Typical debt diseases manifest themselves in different forms in different economies:

Japan's "balance sheet recession": Prolonged deflation after asset bubbles burst, leading to debt overhangs and stagnant growth.

Latin America's debt crises: Recurring cycles of sovereign defaults and stagflation, exacerbated by dollar-denominated external debt.

Europe's sovereign debt crisis: Driven by a monetary union without fiscal integration, creating imbalances between centralized monetary policy and decentralized fiscal policies.

Debt cycle theory states that the driving force of economic growth has shifted from assets to debt and that economic fluctuations have shifted from the asset cycle to the debt cycle. Debt has become an important driver of global growth and a source of instability. When debt financing becomes scarce, economies are vulnerable to downturns. Governments should therefore strengthen fiscal discipline, control the scale of spending, and optimize the structure of spending. At the same time, they must establish sound debt management, strengthen debt risk monitoring and early warning mechanisms, and identify and mitigate debt risks in a timely manner. Solving the global debt problem requires international cooperation and coordination. Countries need to strengthen political communication and cooperation to jointly address debt risks.

Furthermore, international financial institutions and multilateral development banks should strengthen their support to developing countries to help them tackle their debt problems. For countries already in debt crisis, debt restructuring and debt relief measures can be used to reduce their debt burden. These include measures such as extending repayment deadlines, reducing interest rates, and canceling certain debts. At the same time, a robust debt restructuring and relief mechanism should be put in place to ensure its fairness and effectiveness.

Educational inequalities are also a product of the unequal distribution of global resources. Worldwide, 258 million children, adolescents, and young adults, or 17%, do not attend school. There are significant regional disparities: Sub-Saharan Africa has the highest dropout rate at 31%, followed by Central Asia (21%), while Europe and North America have the lowest rates (3%).[7] For example, at their current learning rate, 15-year-old Brazilian students would need 75 years to reach the average math scores of richer countries, and more than 260 years to reach the average reading scores.[8] Within countries, learning outcomes measured by standardized tests are almost always much worse for people living in poverty. In Mexico, for example, 80% of indigenous children do not acquire basic reading and math skills by the end of primary school and are well below the average for primary school students.[9]

Medical resources constitute a key area of inequality in the global distribution of resources. According to research, the distribution of human resources in dentistry is as follows: the majority of the world's 1.6 million dentists are located in Europe and America, meaning that 69% of the world's dentists serve 27% of the world's population. Only 1% of the world's dentists work in Africa, resulting in significant inequalities in access to dental care, as shown by the population to dental personnel ratio.[10]

In the area of climate, the distribution of impacts and responsibilities for climate change at the international level is also unfair. Climate change has a greater impact on smaller countries, and the main responsibility for these changes should lie with larger countries. However, there is a mismatch between influence, responsibility, and capacity within the international climate system. Several studies analyze the imbalance between

[7] Gallagher, J. E., & Hutchinson, L. (2018). Analysis of human resources for oral health worldwide: Unequal distribution. *International Dental Journal*, 68(3), 183–189.

[8] Filmer, D., Langthaler, M., Stehrer, R., & Vogel, T. (2018). *World Development Report*. The World Bank. https://doi.org/10.1111/padr.12163

[9] Instituto Nacional para la Evaluación de la Educación. (2018). La educación obligatoria en México. Informe 2018. Discussion Paper.

[10] Gallagher, J. E., & Hutchinson, L. (2018). Analysis of human resources for oral health worldwide: Unequal distribution. *International Dental Journal*, 68(3), 183–189. https://doi.org/10.1111/idj.12349

responsibility for climate change or the ability to provide support on the one hand, and the economic impacts of climate change on the other hand. Tol et al. (2004) quantify the inequality of market damage caused by climate change based on the FUND 2.6 model. They conclude that climate change affects the world's poorer populations more severely (expressed as a percentage of GDP loss) because they are more exposed to weather conditions, they are closer to the biophysical and experiential limits of the climate, and their adaptive capacity is lower.[11]

The formula for debt-driven growth in industrialized countries and export-driven growth in emerging markets is not sustainable in the long term. Urbanization, high cost of living, consumer behavior and lifestyles, and lax credit policies have led to an increase in the number of people in debt. The McKinsey Global Institute reports that in the period leading up to the 2000–2007 financial crisis, household debt rose to 125% of disposable income. In the United Kingdom, household debt rose to 150% of income.[12] Debt arises from desires and unnecessary demand.[13] Debt and other financial problems are excessive and uncontrollable and lead to a reduced quality of life[14]; an increase in mental health problems,[15] trauma, stress, depression, and anxiety; poor concentration at work; and loss of self-confidence.[16]

Finally, debt creates an unstable domestic economic system. According to the OECD (2012), high public debt can cause vulnerabilities in the

[11] Tol, R. S., Downing, T. E., Kuik, O. J., & Smith, J. B. (2004). Distribution aspects of climate change impacts. *Global Environmental Change*, 14(3), 259–272. https://doi.org/10.1016/j.gloenvcha.2004.04.007

[12] Dobbs, R., Lund, S., Woetzel, J., & Mutafchieva, M. (2015). *Debt and (Not Much) Deleveraging*. McKinsey Global Institute.

[13] Furqani, H., Fuad, Z., Adha, S. I., & Awalurramadhana, A. (2023). Debt-based economy: A reappraisal of prosperity and crisis. *International Journal of Economics and Financial Issues*, 13(2), 109–114. https://doi.org/10.32479/ijefi.14168

[14] Moore, T., & Fifield, K. (2021). What stresses you out the most? Reader's Digest. https://www.rdasia.com.my/what_stresses_you_out_the_most

[15] Ten Have, M., Tuithof, M., van Dorsselaer, S., De Beurs, D., Jeronimus, B., De Jonge, P., & De Graaf, R. (2021). The bidirectional relationship between debts and common mental disorders: Results from a population-based longitudinal study. *Administration and Policy in Mental Health and Mental Health Services Research*, 48(5), 810–820. https://doi.org/10.1007/s10488-021-01131-9

[16] Turunen, E., & Hiilamo, H. (2014). Health effects of debt: A systematic review. *BMC Public Health*, 14(1), 489. https://doi.org/10.1186/1471-2458-14-489

economy that lead to macroeconomic shocks. This trend raises critical questions about the sustainability of current economic practices and underscores the urgent need for alternative models that prioritize financial health, social justice, and environmental sustainability. Without a fundamental change in the economic model, the risks of economic instability and social unrest could increase, affecting both individuals and society at large.

Export-driven growth is slowing in some countries as their low-cost advantage disappears and their export advantage wanes. The global economy must find new drivers and growth models. For example, with the polarization of income levels, the current growth model is facing difficulties. Belonging to a lower income group also has an impact on households, especially as real average wages have largely stagnated. Finally, China's low-wage advantage is gradually disappearing. Nominal wages have increased by an average of nearly 15% per year since China joined the WTO in 2001.[17]

Currently, the rise of trade protectionism and the intensification of trade conflicts have hindered the liberalization and facilitation of global trade and restricted trade exchanges between countries, which has adversely affected the synergistic development of the global economy. Trade protectionism, a widespread form of international trade policy, aims to restrict imports through tariffs, quotas, subsidies, and non-tariff barriers to protect domestic industries, jobs, and markets. A key argument in favor of protectionism is the protection of domestic industries that are at a competitive disadvantage due to technological gaps, inefficiencies, or size constraints. In 2018, for example, the United States introduced tariffs of up to 25% on steel and aluminum imports, citing national security concerns. Trade protectionist measures such as raising tariffs or setting import quotas can reduce the share of foreign goods in the domestic market, thus giving relief to domestic industries and protecting domestic employment.

The theory of protection of young industries is one of the most important theoretical pillars of trade protectionism. This theory states that some emerging industries may not be able to compete with mature foreign industries in the early stages of their development, but through

[17] Coates, B., Horton, D., & McNamee, L. (2012). China: Prospects for export-driven growth. *Economic Round-Up*, 4, 79–102.

government protectionist policies, these industries can gradually accumulate technology, experience, and market share, eventually becoming internationally competitive industries. Trade protectionism can also be explained by national economic security. In the context of globalization, some countries fear that the influx of foreign goods or services could pose a threat to national economic security by undermining national sovereignty, economic lifelines, or social stability. Therefore, the implementation of trade protectionist measures can maintain national economic security and ensure the independent and sustainable development of the national economy.

Increasing integration has been a driver of economic growth, enabling countries to specialize in goods and services in which they have a comparative advantage. However, growing geopolitical tensions have fueled concerns about a possible shift away from globalization, sometimes referred to as "deglobalization."[18] Indeed, the adoption of protectionist measures aimed at restricting the movement of goods and services through the introduction of tariffs and various non-tariff barriers has seen a notable, albeit modest, increase in the international trade landscape. Geopolitical alignment can influence trade flows, as countries tend to use different trade policies, including tariffs, restrictions, and licensing requirements, with their geopolitical allies than with adversaries. The less aligned geopolitically two countries are, the more likely they are to create trade barriers, and the higher those barriers are likely to be.[19] Trade protectionism tends to hinder the development of global trade. In international trade, countries achieve optimal resource allocation and mutual economic benefits through trade.

However, the implementation of protectionist trade policies disrupts this balance and leads to an increase in trade barriers and a reduction in trade flows. This not only harms the economic interests of individual countries but also hinders the growth and development of the global economy. Trade protectionism also harms consumer interest. With free trade, consumers can enjoy high-quality goods and services from around

[18] Qiu, H., Xia, D., & Yetman, J. (2024). Deconstructing global trade: The role of geopolitical alignment. *BIS Quarterly Review*, September 2024, 33–48. https://www.bis.org/publ/qtrpdf/r_qt2409c.pdf

[19] Qiu, H., Xia, D., & Yetman, J. (2024). Deconstructing global trade: The role of geopolitical alignment. *BIS Quarterly Review*, September 2024, 33–48. https://www.bis.org/publ/qtrpdf/r_qt2409c.pdf

the world at relatively low prices. However, the implementation of protectionist trade policies can lead to restrictions on imports of foreign goods and services, thereby reducing consumer choice and increasing price levels. This not only increases the cost of living for consumers but also reduces their quality of life and level of prosperity. In addition, trade protectionism can easily lead to trade wars and conflicts. International trade is characterized by fierce competition between countries. If one country adopts trade protectionist measures, other countries are likely to retaliate, which can lead to trade wars and conflicts. This not only harms the economic interests of all countries but also undermines the international economic order and stability. Finally, trade protectionism can hinder technological progress and innovation. Under conditions of free trade, countries can learn from each other and borrow advanced technologies and management experience, thus promoting technological progress and innovation.

However, the implementation of protectionist trade policies restricts this exchange and cooperation, leading to a slowdown in technological progress and innovation. This not only affects the pace and quality of economic development of each country but also weakens its competitiveness in the international market. Global trade relations have changed recently. The United States withdrew from the Trans-Pacific Partnership and President Trump began imposing tariffs outside the WTO. This tool was used as part of Trump's "Putting America First" economic strategy to promote American industry, protect domestic products from imports, reduce the trade deficit, and develop the national economy as a whole.[20] These protectionist measures began with the introduction of tariffs, first on solar panels and washing machines in January 2018, then on steel and aluminum in March 2018, and from June 2018 with the introduction of tariffs of 25% on more than 800 categories of Chinese products worth $34 billion.[21] China responded by imposing tariffs on imports from the United States. This trend reflects the complex economic dynamics and geopolitical tensions that have been brewing for several years.

[20] Prelipcean, G., & Bucătar, D. G. (2019). Rising protectionism in the global economy. *Economic Sciences Series*, 19(1), 290–298.

[21] Bekkers, E. (2019). Challenges to the trade system: The potential impact of changes in future trade policy. *Journal of Policy Modeling*, 41(3), 489–506. https://doi.org/10.1016/j.jpolmod.2019.03.016

Alongside this moderate increase in concrete protectionist measures, surveys and opinion polls have repeatedly shown that there is a growing public demand for stronger economic protection. This sentiment has been on the rise since the mid-2000s, when concerns about job losses to foreign competitors, the decline of domestic industries, and the perceived unequal distribution of economic benefits came to the forefront of public discourse. Since the global financial crisis, which rocked the world economy and exposed the weaknesses of interconnected markets, the call for economic protection has grown even stronger. The crisis has fueled fears of economic uncertainty, leading many to believe that stricter trade barriers and policies favoring domestic producers could serve as a shield against further economic hardship. According to a WSJ/NBC News poll conducted on March 10–14, 2018, 25% of the respondents said that the trade war with China would protect American jobs and help the US economy; 26% supported tariffs and believed they would help the average American; and 38% approved of how Trump was handling trade between the United States and other countries.[22]

However, economic theory suggests that protectionist measures do not necessarily improve current conditions. Conventional economic theory suggests that comparative advantages and economies of scale create economic gains through economic efficiency. Protectionist measures such as tariffs often trigger retaliatory measures, leading to a massive decline in foreign trade and a slowdown in global economic growth.[23] Economic theory does not claim that free trade is beneficial for all industries and all people. However, the winners of free trade can afford to compensate the losers. As a result, everyone might be better off because the overall gains are positive.[24] At the same time, protectionism is unlikely to help

[22] Lai, E. L. C. (2019). The US-China trade war, US public opinion, and its impact on China. *Economic and Political Studies*, 7(2), 169–184. https://doi.org/10.1080/20954816.2019.1595330

[23] Park, S. C. (2018). US protectionism and trade imbalance between the US and Northeast Asian countries. *International Organisations Research Journal*, 13(2), 76–100.

[24] Rosen, H. F. (2008). Strengthening trade adjustment assistance. Peterson Institute for International Economics No. PB08-2. https://core.ac.uk/download/pdf/6603363.pdf

correct current account imbalances. Furthermore, countries that implement protectionist measures should expect a deterioration in their international competitiveness, which would further undermine the potential for longer-term real GDP growth.[25]

According to Caballero, Farhi, and Gourinchas (2021), global interest rates have fallen to extremely low levels, and the room for further downward adjustment is limited. They develop a model to analyze the effects of currency and trade wars on global equilibrium in this case. They call the downward rigidity of the key interest rate a "zero lower bound" (ZLB), which has become a natural tipping point. Outside the ZLB, the real interest rate clears the global asset market: a shock that leads to a shortage of assets at the current real interest rate causes an endogenous decline in the global real interest rate and restores equilibrium in the global asset market. At the ZLB, the real interest rate can no longer fulfill its equilibrium function. Global production must adjust to clear the asset market. As global production declines, global net demand for assets also declines and the global asset market returns to equilibrium. The role of capital flows also changes at the ZLB because current account surpluses spread low interest rates from the country of origin to the rest of the world. At the ZLB, current account surpluses aggravates recessions. In a global liquidity trap, global production must decline, but the exchange rate influences the distribution of economic downturns among countries. This creates fertile ground for direct intervention in the exchange rate market to boost a country's production, improve its current account balance, and achieve a "beggar-thy-neighbor" zero-sum devaluation at the expense of others. In international trade, a beggar-thy-neighbor economic policy is one that benefits the country that implements it while harming that country's neighbors or trading partners. It usually takes the form of some kind of trade barrier imposed on the neighbors or trading partners or a devaluation of the domestic currency to gain competitive advantage over them. Such a "beggar-thy-neighbor" policy could lead to a currency war. For the same reason, countries have an incentive to wage a trade war by raising tariffs to shift global demand from foreign to domestic goods. However, Caballero, Farhi, and Gourinchas (2021) conclude that trade wars, like currency wars, merely redistribute a global shortage of aggregate demand

[25] Bussière, M., Pérez-Barreiro, E., Straub, R., & Taglioni, D. (2011). Protectionist responses to the crisis: Global trends and implications. *The World Economy*, 34(5), 826–852. https://doi.org/10.1111/j.1467-9701.2011.01355.x

without addressing the underlying cause, which lies in global financial markets.[26]

4.3 Industrial Revival and Policy Adjustment

Policy adjustments made by major powers in response to global imbalances shape the global situation in many ways. These policies, driven by unique economic, political, and geopolitical considerations, form a network of butterfly effects and interdependencies in which the actions of one nation can have repercussions across the world and influence the decisions and courses of others. Emerging and established powers are particularly sensitive to each other's policies. Judgments about the political intentions of others can significantly influence policy responses and lead to different outcomes, such as global peace and stability or the escalation of confrontations.

The COVID-19 pandemic majorly disrupted global value chains and underscored the critical importance of autonomy in industrial production processes, particularly in the healthcare, food, and energy sectors.[27] The manufacturing industry has specific characteristics, such as close forward and backward links, static and dynamic economies of scale, and the ability to quickly adopt and diffuse technological advances. These characteristics enable productivity gains in manufacturing and related services to spread throughout the economy and increase long-term growth potential.[28] Emerging and developing countries were hit hard by the pandemic, but their economies are resilient.

As the global economy recovers, foreign demand in these countries will gradually improve, and internal structural reforms will support growth. Emerging and developing countries in Asia have led global growth. However, challenges remain in emerging and developing countries,

[26] Caballero, R. J., Farhi, E., & Gourinchas, P. O. (2021). Global imbalances and zero-sum policy wars. *The Review of Economic Studies*, 88(6), 2570–2621. https://doi.org/10.1093/restud/rdab015

[27] Sheng, E. L., & Yin, Y. (2024). Coordinating crisis management: The European Union's health policy response to COVID-19. *Health Care: Current Reviews*, 12(3), 409. https://doi.org/10.35248/2375-4273.24.12.409

[28] Feijó, C., Feil, F., & Teixeira, F. A. (2024). Reindustrialization in the context of the Convention on Sustainable Development. *Brazilian Journal of Political Economy*, 44(4), e243626.

where inflationary pressures are systematically higher than in advanced economies. Global inflation is expected to continue to decline in the future, but inflationary pressures in emerging and developing countries remain high.

The COVID-19 pandemic exposed the vulnerability of global industrial and supply chains. To mitigate risks, countries have embarked on rebuilding their industrial and supply chains, but this process can lead to problems such as cost increases and efficiency losses. In addition, geopolitical turmoil can affect the stability of global industrial and supply chains.

For example, ongoing tensions in the Middle East and uncertainties related to the conflict between Russia and Ukraine could lead to lower energy supplies, higher international transportation costs, and higher prices for food, energy, and other raw materials, which would increase price volatility in global commodity markets. Kaldor analyzes the impact of manufacturing on economic growth from a Keynesian perspective. According to Kaldor's first law, the real GDP growth rate depends on the growth of manufacturing. In his model, manufacturing is the sector with the highest static and dynamic returns to scale, the highest productivity gains, and the highest capital accumulation.[29]

Industrialization, reindustrialization, and deindustrialization are defined by changes in the share of manufacturing in GDP and/or domestic employment.[30] "Reindustrialization" refers to a country's strategic efforts to revive and strengthen its industrial sector, with a focus on expanding its production capacity. This initiative has several objectives: to create jobs, to boost production, and to reduce dependence on external sources of goods and materials. By revitalizing their industrial base, countries hope to improve their economic resilience, drive innovation, and ensure greater self-sufficiency.

One example is the Brazilian economy, which has experienced increasing deindustrialization and specialization in the production of resource-intensive goods since the 2000s. The reindustrialization of the

[29] Moczadlo, R. (2020). Re-industrialization to promote growth and employment in the European Union. *Ekonomski vjesnik/Econviews: Review of Contemporary Business, Entrepreneurship and Economic Issues*, 33(1), 39–58.

[30] Tregenna, F. (2011). Manufacturing productivity, deindustrialization, and reindustrialization. WIDER working paper no. 2011/57.

2020s is driving the transformation of production by reviving the country's productivity and competitiveness through investments in fixed assets and R&D. Investments in sustainable industrial processes and advanced technologies have the potential to reduce the environmental impact of industrial production, create high-quality jobs, and improve the competitiveness of Brazilian products in global markets, thus helping to reduce external constraints on economic growth.

The US reindustrialization strategy is one of the typical policy adjustment practices in the context of global industrial revitalization. This strategy aims to revive the national manufacturing industry and improve industrial competitiveness by promoting the return and development of the manufacturing industry. To implement its reindustrialization strategy, the US government has taken a number of policy adjustment measures: (1) increase investment in scientific and technological innovation and R&D, and promote the development of the manufacturing industry toward high-end, intelligent, and environmentally friendly; (2) optimize the distribution of industrial structure and promote the relocation of enterprises to the interior and rural areas; and (3) strengthen international trade cooperation and trade exchanges to promote the coordinated development of global manufacturing.

In recent years, the US government has actively supported and promoted domestic production through various policy measures and initiatives. These include incentives for manufacturers to invest in new technologies, tax breaks, and support for workforce development programs aimed at equipping workers with the skills needed for modern industrial jobs. In addition, as part of reindustrialization efforts, there is an increasing emphasis on sustainable practices to ensure that environmental considerations are integrated into production processes. Such strategic efforts aim to promote economic growth and strengthen national security by minimizing dependence on foreign supply chains. As global markets continue to evolve, the push toward reindustrialization is an important response to the challenges of globalization, technological progress, and changing economic dynamics. For example:

- The CHIPS and Science Act encourages localized production of semiconductors for national security reasons.
- The Inflation Reduction Act allocates $60 billion for clean energy production, including domestic production of solar panels, wind turbines, and batteries.

- The American Nuclear Infrastructure Act of 2021 aims to restore US global leadership in nuclear energy and revitalize the country's nuclear energy supply chain infrastructure.
- For a vehicle to be sold tariff-free in the region, the United States–Mexico–Canada Agreement requires that at least 75% of the vehicle's components be manufactured in North America.[31]

According to a report by Capgemini, the strategic use of legislation and incentives by governments has triggered the development of various frameworks and initiatives designed to promote industrial growth and innovation. These policy measures often include strong incentives for domestic production to strengthen local industry and reduce dependence on imports.

In addition, regulatory processes are being streamlined to create a more flexible and efficient business environment that encourages companies to invest in the country and expand their activities. Targeted industrial investments, particularly in areas considered critical to national strategic interests, such as semiconductors, batteries, renewable energy, defense, and pharmaceuticals, underscore the US government's commitment to a strong domestic industrial base. The United States' commitment to reindustrialization is not just a pipe dream; it is expected to translate into major investments.

Capgemini Research predicts a significant increase in cumulative investments over the next three years, totaling an impressive $1.4 trillion. This financial commitment represents a concerted effort to rebuild and revitalize the nation's industrial sector to improve its competitiveness in the global market. Reindustrialization requires a significant allocation of capital to modernize equipment, advance technologies, and promote workforce skills. This three-pronged investment is essential to modernize manufacturing processes, increase productivity, and foster innovation. However, the total cost of ownership associated with reindustrialization efforts is becoming increasingly complex and multifaceted. Factors such as increasing wages due to skills shortages, rising transportation costs due to supply chain disruptions and inflation, and import tariffs on goods from traditional offshore manufacturing centers are gradually eroding the

[31] Manufacturing resilience: Reindustrialization in the United States. Capgemini. https://www.capgemini.com/us-en/insights/research-library/manufacturing-resilience-reindustrializatinin-the-united-states/

initial cost advantages expected from domestic production. Addressing these challenges requires a nuanced approach that balances the benefits of reindustrialization with effective management of associated costs. Governments and businesses must seek innovative solutions, including partnerships, public–private collaboration, and technological advancements, to offset these rising costs and ensure the long-term viability and success of their reindustrialization efforts.

The Trump administration implemented a series of economic policy measures with distinctive features. In the area of trade, the Trump administration took aggressive protectionist measures. It often fueled trade conflicts and attempted to protect domestic industries through measures such as the imposition of tariffs. Although these measures aimed to protect American jobs and companies, they disrupted the established global trade order and provoked reactions from trading partners. In the area of tax policy, the Trump administration implemented a comprehensive tax cut program designed to boost domestic economic growth and attract businesses to the United States.

However, this approach led to an increase in the budget deficit, raising concerns about the long-term sustainability of such measures. The trade measures taken by Trump were in line with the unilateralist orientation of American foreign policy, showing a preference for a unilateral approach that weakens the international system to the detriment of multilateral mechanisms.[32] Overall, the Trump administration's economic policy, characterized by a strong emphasis on protectionism and unilateralism, has had both intended and unintended consequences for the global economy and the role of the United States in the international community. Although these policies aimed to promote domestic economic interests, they also raised questions about the long-term implications for global trade, fiscal responsibility, and the health of the international system.

When the Biden administration took office, a remarkable shift in economic policy occurred. On trade policy, while the administration did not completely abandon the tough stance that characterized the Trump era, it placed greater emphasis on resolving trade disputes through multilateral mechanisms. This approach aimed to reshape the US leadership role in global trade by promoting cooperation and addressing issues

[32] Sheng, L., & do Nascimento, D. F. (2021). *Love and Trade War: China and the US in Historical Context*. Palgrave MacMillan.

within a multi-country framework, thereby strengthening US influence in a complex international environment. This strategy also reflected the desire to build fairer and more sustainable trade relations in the future.

On the fiscal policy front, the Biden administration unveiled a massive stimulus package to mitigate the economic impact of the COVID-19 pandemic. This package not only provided direct financial support to individuals and businesses but also included large investments in infrastructure and green energy initiatives, all aimed at promoting economic recovery and long-term growth. However, these ambitious measures raised concerns about inflation and debt sustainability. Experts feared that the significant increase in government spending could put upward pressure on prices and lead to an increase in government debt. As a result, the Biden administration faced the challenge of striking a delicate balance between stimulating economic growth and controlling inflation—a dilemma that will undoubtedly influence future economic policy decisions and the broader economic landscape.

Many politicians and decision-makers from both major parties in the United States have explicitly set the reindustrialization of the US economy as a goal, recognizing its critical importance for national growth, job creation, and global competitiveness. However, they propose very different strategies to achieve this goal. The Biden administration, in particular, embarked on a multi-pronged path toward reindustrialization and took a series of legislative measures that included significant spending initiatives and various subsidies to revitalize domestic industries. These legislative efforts are evident in measures such as the CHIPS Act, which focused on promoting semiconductor production, the Infrastructure Investment and Jobs Act, which aimed to modernize the country's infrastructure, and, most notably, the Inflation Reduction Act, which focused on climate. This comprehensive approach not only addressed immediate economic challenges but also focused on long-term sustainability and resilience in the face of global challenges. Through massive investments in green technologies and renewable energy sources, the government aimed to foster innovation and attract talent to emerging sectors, ultimately creating a more robust and self-sufficient economy. These ambitious initiatives reflect the US government's growing recognition that reindustrialization is essential to maintaining the country's economic strength and technological leadership on the global stage.

Reindustrialization is becoming increasingly important in industrialized countries, and manufacturing is once again becoming a priority in the

European Union's economic policy documents.[33] To stimulate and revive the EU economy and competitiveness after the 2008 crisis, EU economic policy began to focus on reindustrialization, particularly in post-socialist member states. In 2010, the European Union announced the Europe 2020 strategy, which aims to achieve smart, sustainable, and inclusive economic growth. To this end, the European Commission presented, among other things, a proposal for a general restructuring of European industrial policy.[34] Although industrial policy was one of the flagships of the Europe 2020 strategy, "Industrial Policy in the Globalized Era," no concrete targets to be achieved were set at that time. In the European Commission's communication two years later, a clear target was set: the share of industry in GDP should increase from around 15% at that time to at least 20% by 2020, while playing an important role in economic growth and job creation. This means that (re)industrialization has become a crucial element of European economies.[35]

Russia is also pursuing a policy of industrial recovery. Since the 1990s, Russia has pursued a liberal monetary economic policy, which has led to a sharp decline in industrial production, reduced economic stability, and increasing dependence on foreign capital, technology, and consumer and non-consumer goods. Today, Russia is heavily dependent on imports, even in strategically important sectors.[36] It is therefore fair to say that the country's sustainable development is threatened by the inadequate development of its domestic industrial production. For example, the value of imports in the machine tool industry and light industry is over 90%, while the value of imports in sectors such as heavy machinery, radio electronics, and medical technology is over 80%. Unfortunately, the situation in other fundamental sectors of the Russian economy, such as food,

[33] Nagy, B., Lengyel, I., & Udvari, B. (2020). Reindustrialization patterns in post-socialist EU member states: A comparative study between 2000 and 2017. *The European Journal of Comparative Economics*, 17(2), 253–275. http://dx.doi.org/10.25428/1824-2979/202002-253-275

[34] Landesmann, M. A. (2015). Industrial policy: Its role in the European economy. *Intereconomics*, 50(3), 133–138.

[35] Nagy, B., Lengyel, I., & Udvari, B. (2020). Reindustrialization patterns in post-socialist EU member states: A comparative study between 2000 and 2017. *The European Journal of Comparative Economics*, 17(2), 253–275. http://dx.doi.org/10.25428/1824-2979/202002-253-275

[36] Gu, X.H., & Sheng, L. (2010) A sensible tool for Pareto-improvement: Capital Controls. Journal of World Trade, 44(3), 567–590.

mining, energy, and communications, is similar, if not more serious. In 2000, for example, Russia imported machinery, equipment, and vehicles worth $10 billion. These figures show that Russia is now heavily dependent on imports. Russia is currently trying to promote industrial revitalization through scientific and technological innovation to overcome the current economic situation and geopolitical tensions.

Industrial revitalization and political adjustment are at the forefront of this global adjustment, which is also reflected in the outsourcing market. Annual outsourcing statistics show that in 2019, the value of outsourced services worldwide reached $92.5 billion. This market grew by just over 8% compared with 2018. Nevertheless, the value of outsourced services provided worldwide remained well below the record level of $104.6 billion in 2014.[37] In addition, the Fourth Industrial Revolution (Industry 4.0), which is based on digitalization, could have a significant impact on the manufacturing industry, and technological developments could lead to the emergence of "connected smart factories." The Fourth Industrial Revolution is also likely to trigger a process of deindustrialization, in which the share of manufacturing in employment is likely to decline further, while productivity is likely to increase or at least not decline due to technological change. These processes are likely to have different effects in industrialized and developing countries and to contribute to the emergence of new divisions of labor.

Germany's "Industry 4.0" strategy is another typical example of policy adjustment in the wake of the global industrial renaissance. This strategy aims to drive forward the modernization and transformation of the manufacturing industry by promoting smart manufacturing and digital transformation. To implement this "Industry 4.0" strategy, the German government has taken a number of policy adjustment measures: (1) increasing investment in scientific and technological innovation and R&D and promote the development of smart manufacturing and digital transformation; (2) strengthening international cooperation and exchanges to promote the coordinated development of global manufacturing industry; and (3) improving the system of laws, regulations, and standards to institutionally ensure smart manufacturing and digital transformation.

In addition, countries have implemented fiscal, monetary, and digital economic adjustments. In response to the economic shock caused by

[37] *Outsourcing Statistics 2024: In the US and Worldwide*. TeamStage. https://teamstage.io/outsourcing-statistics/

the COVID-19 pandemic, governments adopted fiscal stimulus measures, which led to an increase in global debt. In 2025, global debt risks have become a major obstacle to economic growth. At the same time, loose monetary policy has led to inflationary pressures. Central banks face the challenge of adjusting their monetary policy to strike a balance between economic growth and price stability. In terms of fiscal stimuli, governments stimulate economic growth by increasing public spending, cutting taxes and fees, and taking other measures. However, these measures increase government debt. To control debt risks, governments must formulate sound fiscal policies to ensure the sustainability and controllability of debt. In terms of monetary policy, central banks stimulate economic growth by lowering interest rates, providing liquidity support, and taking other measures. However, these measures lead to inflationary pressures. To achieve a balance between economic growth and price stability, central banks must carefully adjust their monetary policy to avoid the negative effects of excessive easing or tightening on the economy. To reduce the vulnerability of global industrial and supply chains, countries have initiated the reconstruction of industrial and supply chains. However, this process can bring problems such as higher costs and lower efficiency. To address these challenges, countries must strengthen regional cooperation and work together to promote the stability and security of industrial and supply chains. For example, the signing of the RCEP will help promote economic growth in the Asia–Pacific region. By strengthening regional cooperation, countries can jointly address the vulnerability of global industrial and supply chains and improve their resilience and stability. There is now a global consensus on combating climate change and promoting green, low-carbon development. In 2025, the green economy became a new pole of economic growth, and related industries and companies are expected to experience rapid development. As major sources of carbon emissions, industries must focus on green and low-carbon transformation as they recover. The COVID-19 pandemic accelerated the global digital transformation, and the digital economy has become a new engine of economic growth. In 2025, new technologies such as artificial intelligence, 5G, and the IoT offer more opportunities for the global economy.

Looking ahead, the political trajectories of major countries may continue to diverge. As countries adjust their policies, their approaches could evolve toward a new equilibrium that promotes a more balanced and inclusive global economy. However, we may also face a divided and turbulent future, with economic growth slowing and cooperation overshadowed by competition. In this interconnected world, each country's policies are linked not only to its own future but also to that of other countries. As the international community stands at a crossroads, the way forward remains uncertain, and policy adjustments made by different countries could determine the global situation.

4.4 Strategy in the New Global Landscape

Geopolitical tensions and disruptions to global value chains have prompted policymakers to rethink their approach to globalization. In response, many countries are now considering the strategy of "friendshoring," a practice that focuses on trading primarily with nations that share similar values, as a means of minimizing vulnerability to trade weaponization and ensuring access to key inputs. Friendshoring refers to the outsourcing of activities to suppliers located in countries or regions considered friendly. This model aims to strengthen economic ties and promote cooperation with allies, thus improving mutual support in times of crisis. Through friendshoring, countries could reduce supply chain risks to some extent and increase the stability and security of their industries. Friendshoring is now seen as an alternative to a market-based offshoring approach (where operations are relocated to countries with cheap labor). This relocation not only addresses concerns about potential disruptions from geopolitical conflict or trade wars but also encourages increased cooperation between allies, promoting technology sharing and resource integration. As countries rethink their globalization strategies in light of current geopolitical realities, friendshoring is increasingly recognized as an effective way to manage the complexity of the international economic landscape while protecting national interests and ensuring economic resilience. This evolving approach reflects the general trend toward prioritizing security and stability in economic relations and points to a significant shift in the way nations engage in global trade.

To achieve friendly outsourcing, both parties should establish a mechanism to enhance mutual trust, strengthen communication and cooperation, and ensure the smooth operation of the outsourcing process. This includes the establishment of regular communication mechanisms, the exchange of information resources, and joint problem-solving. Both parties should focus on long-term cooperation and avoid short-sighted behavior. The common interests of both parties in the outsourcing process should be ensured by signing long-term contracts and making joint investments. Both parties should also strengthen talent promotion and recruitment to improve the quality and level of the outsourcing process. This includes improving employee training, attracting highly qualified talent, and establishing talent incentive systems. In addition, both parties should actively promote innovation and advance technological R&D as well as industrial modernization. The value added and competitiveness of the outsourcing process should be increased through joint R&D of new products and technologies.

Friendshoring has emerged as a strategic approach that can significantly improve the security and stability of global supply chains. In recent years, the shockwaves of the COVID-19 pandemic, combined with growing geopolitical tensions between Western nations and China and the ongoing war in Ukraine, have significantly disrupted the security of these supply chains. Western countries import large quantities of critical minerals, many of which are controlled by China and, to a lesser extent, Russia, making supply security a key issue for Western governments. In June 2022, the United States, together with its Western allies, took a significant step forward by establishing the Mineral Security Partnership. This initiative underscores the growing importance of building resilient and secure supply chains, particularly for minerals critical to various industries such as technology, energy, and defense. The key point is that while friendshoring could mitigate vulnerabilities in Western supply chains for critical minerals, its effectiveness depends on reducing dependence on China in the context of national and geopolitical security.[38] The more economic sanctions are implemented, the more trade relations become an instrument of foreign and security policy.[39] Ultimately, friendshoring represents a proactive response to a rapidly changing global landscape, aimed at creating a more secure and stable economic environment by cultivating closer relationships with trusted partners while addressing the vulnerabilities that arise from dependence on potentially hostile nations.

The United States actively promotes friendshoring. US Treasury Secretary Janet Yellen outlined Washington's new approach to trade: "Rather

[38] Vivoda, V., & Matthews, R. (2023). "Friend-shoring" as a panacea for vulnerabilities in the West's supply chain for critical minerals. *Mineral Economics*, 37, 463–476. 1–14. https://doi.org/10.1007/s13563-023-00402-1

[39] Maihold, G. (2022). A new geopolitics of supply chains: The rise of friend-shoring. IISS discussion paper.

than becoming heavily dependent on countries with which we have geopolitical tensions and on whose continued, reliable supplies we cannot rely, we need to truly diversify our suppliers." She added, "Friendshoring means that we have a group of countries that adhere strictly to certain norms and values, and that we need to deepen our relationships with these partners and work together to ensure that we can meet our needs for critical materials." The American tech giant Apple recently implemented friendshoring measures and moved part of its iPhone production from China to India. Currently, only 5% of Apple products are manufactured outside of China, highlighting the company's historical dependence on its Chinese supply chain. However, a recent analysis by JP Morgan suggests that this share could reach 25% by 2025 as companies seek to mitigate the risks associated with over-reliance on a single country.[40] This shift not only reflects the changing global trade landscape but also underscores the urgent need for US companies to rethink their supply chains to strengthen their resilience to geopolitical uncertainties and ensure a stable flow of materials critical to their operations. As this trend gains momentum, it could lead to significant changes in the dynamics of global manufacturing and trade partnerships and promote a more interconnected network of nations aligned with US interests and values.

The restructuring of the semiconductor industry is a typical example of friendshoring in the United States. Semiconductors are key components of modern electronic devices and are essential to national security and economic development. However, the US semiconductor industry has long been heavily dependent on external supply chains, particularly for raw materials, manufacturing, packaging, and testing. Faced with the increasingly complex global geopolitical situation, the US government recognized the potential risks of this dependence and decided to act. As part of the "friendly shore outsourcing" strategy, the US government has worked closely with a number of allies and partners to drive the restructuring of the semiconductor supply chain. Particularly noteworthy is the cooperation between the United States and South Korea, Japan, Taiwan, and other countries. These countries and regions have advanced technologies and complete industrial chains in the semiconductor industry and form a good complementary relationship with the United States.

[40] Stefan, E. (2023, February 17). What is the difference between "friendshoring" and other global trade buzzwords? World Economic Forum. https://www.weforum.org/agenda/2023/02/friendshoring-global-trade-buzzwords/

In terms of cooperation between the United States and South Korea, the two countries have long-standing relations in the semiconductor sector. To further strengthen this cooperation, the governments of the two countries have signed a series of agreements aimed at jointly promoting the development and innovation of the semiconductor industry. These agreements cover technological R&D, talent promotion, market access, and other aspects, providing semiconductor companies from both countries with more opportunities for cooperation and room for development.

To promote the restructuring of the semiconductor supply chain, the US government is also focusing on strengthening cooperation with domestic companies. Through financial subsidies, tax incentives, and other policy support measures, the US government encourages domestic semiconductor companies to increase their R&D investments and expand their independent innovation capabilities. At the same time, the US government actively encourages cooperation between domestic semiconductor companies and companies in allied and partner countries to jointly advance technological R&D and market expansion. It is worth noting that the US government has not completely abandoned cooperation with China to promote the restructuring of the semiconductor supply chain.

Despite some challenges and uncertainties in the economic and trade relations between China and the United States, the US government continues to believe that some cooperation with China is necessary to maintain the stability and development of the global semiconductor market. Therefore, while promoting the restructuring of the semiconductor supply chain, the US government is actively seeking opportunities for cooperation with China.

Friendshoring has generated much controversy, particularly regarding corporate costs. In complex supply chains, the short-term relocation of company sites and the shortening of supply chains will have financial implications for companies, be costly, and take a lot of time. It is therefore estimated that up to 26% of global exports could be relocated over the next five years, representing a value of up to $4.6 trillion.[41] The latest empirical findings show that although some countries could benefit from friendshoring if their bloc unilaterally imposes additional trade costs on the other bloc without the latter responding with similar measures,

[41] Maihold, G. (2022). A new geopolitics of supply chains: The rise of friendshoring. IISS discussion paper.

friendshoring is costly for most economies and leads to real production losses of between 0.1 and 4.7% of global GDP.[42] This potential decline in economic output underscores the delicate balance that countries must strike between diversifying their supply chains and managing the risks associated with such transitions. Overall, although friendshoring is an attractive alternative to strengthen supply chain resilience, the financial burdens and long-term economic impacts should not be overlooked, making it a controversial topic in international trade discussions.

The term "Indo-Pacific" emerged in around 2010 as a regional framework for strategic debate in the United States under the Obama administration and became an important regional term in official US rhetoric under the Trump administration until 2017.[43] Historically, the US FOIP focused on security and defense policy. With the shift to the Indo-Pacific, the United States and its partners seek to strengthen their alliances and partnerships, expand their military presence and capabilities, promote economic integration, and advance shared values and interests. For South Asia, in addition to promoting an important defense partnership with India, the aim is to strengthen close cooperation with Sri Lanka, the Maldives, Bangladesh, and Nepal. The same applies to the Southeast Asian countries of Vietnam, Indonesia, Malaysia, Cambodia, Laos, Brunei Darussalam, and the island states of the Western Pacific. The term "Indo-Pacific" itself emphasizes the interconnection of the Indian and Pacific Oceans and underscores the region's strategic importance for global trade, economic growth, and security. The rebalancing strategy takes into account the growing influence of countries such as China in the region and aims to maintain a balance of power that supports international norms and promotes stability. "Indo-Pacific" is a political term and is therefore neither purely descriptive nor value-neutral. In particular, the Trump administration's concept of a "free and open Indo-Pacific" aims to contain China and is thus an expression of the growing strategic rivalry between Washington and Beijing.[44] In Beijing, the "Indo-Pacific"

[42] Javorcik, B., Kitzmueller, L., Schweiger, H., & Yıldırım, M. A. (2024). Economic costs of friendshoring. *The World Economy*, 47(7), 2871–2908. https://doi.org/10.1111/twec.13555

[43] Scott, D. (2018). The Indo-Pacific in US strategy: Responding to power shifts. *Rising Powers Quarterly*, 2(2), 19–43.

[44] Heiduk, F., & Wacker, G. (2020). From Asia-Pacific to Indo-Pacific: significance, implementation and challenges. SWP Research Paper 9.

is therefore primarily understood as a US-led containment strategy against China.

In 2024, the United States reaffirmed its commitment to this strategy with a statement entitled "The United States' Enduring Commitment to the Indo-Pacific: Two Years After the Release of the Administration's Indo-Pacific Strategy." According to the statement, "The United States is an Indo-Pacific nation. As the world's most dynamic and fastest growing region, the Indo-Pacific is a critical engine for America's future security and prosperity."[45] Furthermore, since the release of the Indo-Pacific Strategy in February 2022, the United States has taken historic steps to advance the shared vision of a free, open, connected, prosperous, secure, and resilient Indo-Pacific region. The United States pledged to continue demonstrating leadership and commitment to the Indo-Pacific region, strengthen the region's capabilities and resilience to meet the challenges and opportunities of the twenty-first century, and show that together we can build a better future. In the document, the United States summarizes the achievements of its strategy over the past two years in five areas and states that it will continue to recommend them: promoting a free and open Indo-Pacific; building connections within and beyond the region; promoting regional prosperity; strengthening regional stability; and promoting resilience in the face of twenty-first century transnational threats.

Promoting a free and open Indo-Pacific: This essentially comprises five measures: a commitment to promote a free and open space for private life and an open society; states make their political decisions independently and without coercion; at the regional level, issues are addressed openly, rules are established transparently and applied fairly, and goods, ideas, and people can move freely. These efforts include promoting human rights and democratic institutions worldwide and cooperating with like-minded partners; supporting democracy in Myanmar; countering threats posed by foreign information manipulation and interference; addressing the Rohingya humanitarian crisis; and upholding international maritime law in the South China Sea.

[45] US Department of State. (2024, February 9). The United States' enduring commitment to the Indo-Pacific: Two years since the release of the Administration's Indo-Pacific Strategy. https://www.state.gov/the-united-states-enduring-commitment-to-the-indo-pacific-marking-two-years-since-the-release-of-the-administrations-indo-pacific-strategy/

Building connections within and beyond the region: The United States has strengthened its bilateral relationships, solidified regional architecture, and pooled its collective strength with partners and allies by strengthening an effective and united ASEAN; deepening trilateral cooperation between the United States, Japan, and South Korea; implementing the Quad initiative; mobilizing new resources and expanding the presence in the Indo-Pacific region; recognizing the Cook Islands and Niue; launching the Partners in the Blue Pacific initiative; expanding trilateral cooperation with Japan and the Philippines; strengthening bilateral partnerships with countries in the Indo-Pacific region; supporting India's role as a regional leader; expanding partnerships in the Indian Ocean; connecting European and Atlantic allies to the Indo-Pacific region; and investing in people-to-people relations.

Promoting regional prosperity: The United States prioritizes investments that promote innovation, strengthen economic competitiveness, create well-paying jobs, strengthen supply chains, and expand economic opportunities for all in the Indo-Pacific. To this end, it has deepened its economic engagement by successfully hosting APEC 2023; concluding negotiations on the pillars of the Indo-Pacific Economic Framework (IPEF); building high-quality infrastructure; entering into COFA-related agreements; launching the US–Taiwan 21st Century Trade Initiative; promoting digital connectivity; advancing cooperation on critical and emerging technologies; and co-hosting the Indo-Pacific Economic Forum.

Strengthening regional stability: The United States continues to deepen cooperation, support allies' and partners' investments in their own capabilities, and improve interoperability to promote regional security. It continues to strengthen regional security by supporting the security partnership between Australia, the United Kingdom, and the United States; strengthening security alliances; expanding presence; supporting maritime situational awareness and maritime security; promoting cooperation on cybersecurity and capacity building; supporting Taiwan's self-defense capabilities; strengthening national defense capabilities; combating the circumvention of sanctions against North Korea; and cooperating on civil security issues.

Advancing Resilience in the Face of 21st Century Transnational Threats: Over the past two years, the United States has worked with partners in the Indo-Pacific region to reduce vulnerability to the impacts of climate change, accelerate the transition to clean energy and other critical climate actions, and support investments in global health security. It also promotes regional resilience by supporting climate adaptation and climate resilience in the Pacific Islands and the Maldives; using a clean economy agreement under the Indo-Pacific Economic Framework and a Catalytic Capital Fund; promoting climate goals, clean energy, and energy security; supporting investments in health and climate protection through the Quad and APEC initiatives; and supporting water, land, and forest management.

There are actually two main reasons for this recent shift in strategic language, each with profound implications for the global landscape. The first is geoeconomic in nature and involves a fundamental change in the dynamics of international trade and economic relations. As the global economy has become increasingly globalized, trade volumes have skyrocketed, with a focus on long-distance energy transportation, particularly between the Indian and Pacific oceans. This increasing interconnectedness has reshaped economic dependencies and alliances, necessitating a reassessment of traditional trade routes and partnerships. Nations are now forced to renegotiate their positions in this complex web of economic interactions to maximize their share of lucrative trade while minimizing potential vulnerabilities. The Asia–Pacific region has an impressive presence on the global stage, comprising three of the world's largest economies, seven of the eight fastest growing markets, and 7 of the 10 strongest military forces. Together, their economic output represents an impressive 60% of global GDP, underscoring their central role in the global economy. As evidence of its rapid growth, Asia overtook both North America and Europe in 2015 to become the world's largest economic region. This dominance is underpinned by the region's strategic maritime infrastructure, with 9 of the world's 10 busiest ports located in South and East Asia, facilitating huge international trade and movement of goods.

The second reason for this strategic shift in language lies in geopolitics, an area heavily influenced by the rise of China and, to a lesser but still significant extent, India in the region. Among the various reasons for the Indo-Pacific initiative, the rise of China is the main driving factor.[46] The rise of China, driven by rapid economic growth and comprehensive military modernization, has profoundly altered the balance of power not only in Asia but also on the global stage. China's growing influence has prompted other nations to rethink their strategies and forge new alliances to counter potential threats while seizing opportunities for mutual benefit. According to them, the rise of China has disrupted the strategic balance in Asia, while the rise of the Asian continent means that a potential new Asian model is emerging with China at its center. In particular, China has proposed the Belt and Road Initiative, an initiative that simultaneously encompasses the Indo-Pacific Ocean and the Eurasian continent. For China, avoiding a global economic and/or military confrontation with the United States is a priority. In response, China has adopted a more proactive foreign policy toward its neighbors to prevent them from forming a united front with the United States. This approach underscores China's belief that peaceful coexistence is the best path to sustainable development and regional stability. By cultivating cooperative relations with its neighbors, China seeks to secure its strategic interests while promoting a vision of shared prosperity that resonates throughout the region.

India's growing economic and political importance has further complicated the complex regional situation. India is seeking to expand its sphere of influence and consolidate its position as a major power not only in South Asia but also on the global stage, operating in an environment characterized by fierce competition and shifting alliances. The country's robust economic growth, driven by advances in technology, manufacturing, and services, has made it an important player in regional trade dynamics. This dual geoeconomic and geopolitical shift is particularly noteworthy because it forces neighboring countries to rethink their strategies and pursue more nuanced and adaptable foreign policies.

The policy aims to safely navigate the dangerous waters of an increasingly multipolar world in which power relations are no longer dominated by a single superpower. Nations are now forming strategic partnerships,

[46] Zhang, J. (2019). The US Indo-Pacific Initiative and its implications for China. In Zhu, C.P.: *Annual Report on the Development of the Indian Ocean Region (2018) Indo-Pacific: Definition and Strategic Implementation* (pp. 53–82). https://doi.org/10.1007/978-981-13-7693-1_3

engaging in multilateral dialogues, and seeking to balance their relationships with both India and other key players, including China and the United States. As a result, the region is the scene of a complex interplay between diplomacy, economic cooperation, and security considerations that reflects the challenges and opportunities of this new world order. This changing situation underscores the importance of flexibility and foresight in foreign policy as countries strive to protect their national interests while promoting regional stability and cooperation.

In summary, the Indo-Pacific, as a major geographical and economic hub, underscores the region's crucial role in shaping global dynamics and influencing international relations. Its importance goes far beyond mere economic growth and encompasses essential elements of political cooperation and strategic alignment between nations. The ongoing evolution of the Indo-Pacific landscape is fundamentally changing global relations, particularly the complex and often conflictual interactions between the United States and China. This is not only an economic shift but also a profound political realignment that reflects a changing balance of power within the international system, once dominated by a few major players. As the world's two largest economies engage in a complex confrontation marked by trade disputes, technological competition, and ideological differences, the Indo-Pacific represents a crucial hub.

Here, global cooperation and competition are being redefined, creating a dynamic environment in which alliances and partnerships are constantly shifting. The implications of this changing landscape are far-reaching, affecting regional security, economic partnerships, and the diplomatic strategies of smaller nations caught between these two giants. As the geopolitical chess game continues to evolve, the full impact of these changes on global governance, trade routes, and security structures is not yet clear. This places the Indo-Pacific region at the center of future international developments and makes it a barometer for assessing global trends in cooperation and conflict.

Beyond the Asia–Pacific region, geopolitical conflicts continue to arise around the world. With globalization and profound shifts in national interests, international geopolitical tensions and conflicts are increasingly becoming the focus of global attention. From the ongoing conflict between Russia and Ukraine to the escalating conflict in the Middle East and security risks in the Asia–Pacific region, many parts of the world are in turmoil and the security situation is precarious.

The conflict between Russia and Ukraine is undoubtedly one of the hotspots of current geopolitical tensions. The conflict has been going on for some time now and has had devastating consequences for Russia and Ukraine, as well as for the future of security in Europe. Both sides have invested heavily and the war has spread, resulting in numerous casualties and high consumption of resources. Eastern Ukraine has become a battlefield, people have been displaced, and repeated international calls for a ceasefire have been largely ignored.

The conflict between Russia and Ukraine is not only a military confrontation between the two countries but also a contest between Russia and the West, especially NATO members. Western countries have imposed a series of economic sanctions on Russia while providing military and political support to Ukraine. This has led to a significant shift in the global geopolitical order, with serious implications for European security in particular. *The Economist* reports that the conflict between Russia and Ukraine has plunged the world into its most chaotic security situation since World War II and that the confrontation between global camps has intensified. The world has experienced the greatest division of countries since the end of the Cold War and the most intense wave of sanctions and counter-sanctions in history. The Russia–Ukraine conflict has also exacerbated geopolitical tensions worldwide and further deteriorated relations between Russia and the West, with the two sides maneuvering against each other on several fronts. For example, the escalation of the military confrontation between Russia and NATO in the Baltic and Black Seas has exacerbated the security situation in Europe. At the same time, the conflict has caused turmoil in global energy markets, driving up oil and natural gas prices and profoundly affecting the global economy.

The Middle East has always been a geopolitical hotspot. In recent years, conflicts and unrest have increased. The conflict between Israel and several Arab countries has escalated, and the Israeli–Palestinian issue is once again the focus of international attention. The Arab response to Israel's aggressive foreign policy, which has triggered regional tensions, is at its peak. The Israeli–Palestinian conflict is not only a confrontation between Israel and the Palestinians but also includes the conflict between Hezbollah in Lebanon, the Houthis in Yemen, and Israel, as well as the potential conflict between Israel and Iran. The spillover effects of these conflicts have made the situation in the Middle East more complex and volatile. Israel's military operations in the Gaza Strip and its attacks in Syria, Iran, and Lebanon have demonstrated its firm stance in regional conflicts. This stance could further escalate tensions in the Middle East and pose a challenge to the global governance system.

In addition, conflicts in the Middle East have led to high numbers of casualties and refugee flows. These refugee problems not only place a heavy burden on the Middle East region but also pose major challenges to the international community. At the same time, conflicts in the Middle East have triggered turbulence in the global energy market and changes in the geopolitical landscape. For example, oil price volatility and tensions in natural gas markets are closely linked to these conflicts. Besides these regions, geopolitical tensions exist in other parts of the world. In South Asia, for example, territorial disputes and religious conflicts between India and Pakistan have not been satisfactorily resolved. Similarly, in Africa, there are territorial disputes and ethnic conflicts in some countries. In South America, political unrest in countries such as Venezuela is fueling regional geopolitical tensions. The spread of these geopolitical tensions not only affects regional stability and development but also poses serious challenges to the international community.

Conclusion

Global economic imbalances are a multifaceted phenomenon involving macroeconomic policies, industrial structures, and the complex web of globalization. Turmoil in global financial markets and geopolitical instability have become the main challenges of today's global economy. The United States and China, as twin pillars of the global economic landscape, carry considerable weight in determining the stability and balance of the global economy. The policies adopted by these two economic powers, including their fiscal strategies, trade regulations, approaches to foreign investment, play a crucial role in shaping global economic dynamics. Moreover, their respective development trajectories, shaped by different political ideologies, economic models, and historical contexts, have profound implications for the overall health of the global economy. This book explored the causes, mechanisms, and sustainable solutions to global imbalances by analyzing the economic disparities between China and the United States and their impact on the global landscape. From differences in industrial structures and trade dynamics to policy adjustments and geopolitical factors, the emergence of global imbalances is multidimensional and requires comprehensive strategies to address them.

Global imbalances not only distort the distribution of resources but also trigger several chain reactions. First, the US current account deficit relies on capital inflows to be sustainable, and any reversal of capital flows could trigger a global financial crisis. The 2008 financial crisis and capital outflows during the COVID-19 pandemic are examples of

E. Li Sheng, *A Recent History of Global Imbalances*,
https://doi.org/10.1007/978-981-95-1834-0

this vulnerability. Second, offshore outsourcing by developed countries has led to the loss of manufacturing jobs, exacerbating inequality at home. For example, deindustrialization in the United States has led some regions to become trapped in rural poverty zones, while developing countries are caught in the technological upgrade trap. Finally, geopolitical tensions, the resurgence of trade protectionism, and strategies such as friendshoring have exacerbated economic rivalries between nations. Currently, trade between China and the United States is fraught with inevitable frictions, primarily due to China's relentless pursuit of economic progress and the United States' vigilant stance against perceived threats to its long-standing economic dominance. These frictions manifest themselves in various forms, including trade tariffs, export restrictions, and intense competition for technological innovation. Ongoing trade tensions exacerbate misunderstandings and increase the risk of retaliation, creating a conflictual atmosphere that hampers constructive dialogue. This conflict prevents both nations from realizing their desired macroeconomic visions, because their focus on external adversaries distracts them from addressing fundamental internal constraints resulting from unbalanced domestic economic systems. For example, the United States faces growing trade deficits, income inequality, and changing labor markets, while China faces overcapacity and environmental degradation. These frictions not only affect bilateral relations but also have broader implications for the global economy, as other countries may find themselves caught between the two economic giants. The excessive concentration of resources in a limited number of countries and the unsustainability of debt-driven growth models thus represent long-term vulnerabilities for the global economy. The ongoing conflict is hampering cooperation on key global issues such as climate change, public health, and sustainable development. In this complex landscape, it is becoming increasingly urgent for both nations to find common ground and pursue cooperative strategies, as failure to do so could jeopardize global economic stability and growth.

To correct the imbalances between the United States and China, dual-track cooperation, a promising but difficult approach, requires mutual adjustments. For China, this means embarking on a path toward less government intervention in various sectors, which would help develop a more dynamic and innovative market-oriented economy. Such a transformation would require not only the implementation of market reforms but also a cultural shift that encourages entrepreneurship, innovation, and competition so that private enterprises can thrive and drive economic growth. At the same time, the United States must work to overcome the deep partisan divides that have hindered effective governance in the past. Developing economic policies with a clear, long-term vision is essential to address the country's economic vulnerabilities, such as income inequality, regional disparities, and job losses. This policy will not only contribute to domestic stability but will also strengthen the country's role in promoting global cooperation. By engaging in multilateral frameworks, the United States can strengthen its economic position while contributing to global stability. In addition, both nations must recognize the interconnectedness of their economies and the broader global landscape and understand that cooperation in areas such as trade, technology, and climate change is essential for mutual benefit. The path to effective dual-track cooperation will undoubtedly require patience, compromise, and sustained dialogue, but the potential rewards of greater economic resilience and shared progress are well worth the effort.

Unfortunately, imbalances between China and the United States will persist and could worsen over time if nationalist sentiments gain strength. The rise in nationalism could lead to protectionist policies and trade barriers, further straining economic relations and fostering a climate of mistrust. As each nation seeks to prioritize its own interests, there is a growing risk that cooperative efforts will diminish, leading to more competition rather than increased cooperation. These growing tensions will not only complicate bilateral relations but also threaten to undermine the delicate balance required for sustainable global economic development. The interconnectedness of today's global economy means that disruptions in one major economy can ripple across the world, affecting supply chains, investment flows, and market stability. Moreover, as both countries pursue their individual goals, important issues such as climate change, public health, and technological progress could be sidelined, leading to collective inefficiencies in responding to global challenges.

An examination of the causes of global imbalances, the structural effects of deindustrialization in developed countries, and offshore outsourcing to developing countries, combined with an analysis of the experiences of developed countries such as the United States, sheds light on the multifaceted approach needed to restore global economic balance. The international community, including China and the United States, must unite in a concerted and collaborative effort. This unity is essential because it involves not only the creation but also the strengthening of effective international systems and norms that can facilitate fair trade practices and equitable economic relations among nations.

In addition, improving policy coordination across borders is essential, as it ensures that countries work together to tackle common challenges, thereby promoting stability and shared growth. Furthermore, the launch of structural reforms in individual economies is an important step toward sustainable development. Developed countries must reduce their dependence on consumption-driven models and restore the competitiveness of their manufacturing sector through reindustrialization measures such as the CHIPS Act in the United States and the Industry 4.0 initiative in the European Union. Developing countries should promote industrial modernization and increase domestic demand. For example, China needs to evolve from the "world's factory" to a "smart manufacturing powerhouse" while improving social security to reduce the savings rate.

Reform of the international monetary and trade system is of crucial importance. Promoting the diversification of the international monetary system reduces dependence on the US dollar, while improving global trade rules can prevent protectionism. For example, regional cooperation frameworks such as the RCEP and IPEF can promote fair trade practices. Tackling climate change and the debt crisis requires transnational cooperation, for example through reforms within the IMF and the World Bank. Building resilient supply chains through friendshoring strategies must avoid bloc fragmentation.

It is worth noting that deindustrialization and outsourcing practices by developed countries have imposed significant environmental burdens and ecological costs on developing countries downstream in their supply chains. As a result, technological innovation and a green transition have become essential. Investing in green technologies, as demonstrated by the Inflation Control Act, can simultaneously promote economic growth and environmental sustainability. Digitalization and smart manufacturing, such as the German Industry 4.0 initiative, can improve the efficiency of global industrial chains.

Such reforms should focus on creating stronger economic frameworks that prioritize inclusion and equity and enable all parts of society to benefit from economic progress. By working together, nations can harness the collective power of global cooperation and leverage diverse resources and expertise to address the root causes of economic imbalance. It is imperative that countries not only recognize their interdependence but also actively engage in dialogue and partnership. This collaborative approach can promote a resilient and prosperous future for all nations involved, as well as for the global community as a whole.

Index

E. Li Sheng, *A Recent History of Global Imbalances*,
https://doi.org/10.1007/978-981-95-1834-0

FSC
www.fsc.org
MIX
Papier | Fördert
gute Waldnutzung
FSC® C083411

Kolibri 360 GmbH
Ferdinand-Jühlke-Straße 7
99095 Erfurt, Deutschland
produktsicherheit@kolibri360.de